Testimonials

"Kath traverses her professional vocation with profound pride, precision and technical depth of understanding. Yet industry experience alone is not the only key to Kath's (and her clients') beautiful bounties of abundance, manifestation, success and recurring blessing." (excerpt from Holistic Bliss Magazine, October 2020)

— Andrew Dudek
Former journalist and lawyer, director and producer
Gee You! Films Pty Ltd (SA)

"Your money mindset impacts almost every aspect of your life, and in this book, Kath Orman draws on her experience and success as a financial adviser and lifestyle coach to gently guide you through discovering your money mindset and, more importantly, she provides practical and proven strategies to move you closer to living the life you want and deserve."

— David Penglase
Behavioural scientist and author of *Living in the Light of Day*

"We've been a part of the Goals & Dreams family for quite a while now. Kath and the team have always taken the time in both a professional and friendly manner to prepare us for every step of the journey towards our hopes and adventures."

— S & T B (Lawnton, QLD)

"Kath is unique. Her kind and caring soul shines through in her relationships with her clients. We feel very fortunate and valued as her clients."

— S & D M (Redcliffe, QLD)

"I have known Kath for nearly 30 years, and she has assisted me with my long-term financial planning for most of that time. She has the unique ability to not only see things from my lens but also understand why I see things that way. Her professionalism and business acumen are second to none."

— K M (Auchenflower, QLD)

"Goals & Dreams is the perfect brand for Kath. Good leadership requires a vision, a positive attitude and an ability to inspire people to take action. This sums up Kath and her business."

—S & J P (Scarborough, QLD)

"Kath has shown me the fun side to money: to not spend every second working for a never-ending goal, to go out and enjoy life, to take a holiday and to create experiences as well as fortunes. Three years ago, I had a meeting with Kath. She said, 'Mitch, I am going to give you the same advice as I give my retiree clients. Go out and have fun. You have put in the hard yards, go and enjoy yourself.' From that moment on, it changed my perspective on money and life. It changed how I focus my time. Instead of making money and wealth, I now create experiences and fortunes. You can't take money to your grave, but you can take memories and experiences. Working three different jobs in three different fields, I was unsure of my end goal and my financial future. With Kath's help, she focused my direction and allowed me to free my time while still creating a grounding financial future for myself. For that I am extremely grateful."

— M E (Boondall, QLD)

"We were delighted to find Kath when we sought her out to assist us with our future financial needs as we approached retirement age. We have been with Kath for 15 years. Without a doubt, this was the best decision we have made and have always found that she looks after our finances as if they were her own. Her positive attitude always inspires us, and her ever-growing team reflect this as well. We are looking forward to many more years with her guidance. From the start she quickly became a true friend who can always be relied on."

— B & A J (Perth, WA)

"We came to Kath with what we had managed to save and Kath made it grow. Before talking to Kath, we were very concerned about how we were going to continue to have a regular income but, with her extensive knowledge and calming influence, I now know that we will continue to be financially secure. Naturally, at our age and with ongoing health concerns, we are aware that eventually there will be only one of us to carry on. Knowing that Kath is there to help is very reassuring."

— D & E B (Carseldine, QLD)

"Kath is an amazing woman of many talents. She is more than our financial adviser. Kath is passionate and has a spiritual inclination to help others achieve their goals and dreams through sound financial advice. We have found Kath to be genuinely caring and happy, and always ready with a hug and a smile. She is generous with the annual Christmas party, wine tours and other events that we get to enjoy as clients. We consider ourselves to be truly blessed to have Kath in our lives."

— R & R C (Jindalee, QLD)

"We started considering retirement about two years before we ended up following through with it. We made an appointment with Kath and talked in length about what the future would look like financially for us. We finally had a plan put in place with Kath's help and went about starting to work towards our 'independence day'. When we decided to think seriously about pulling the pin on our working life, we contacted Kath who waved her magic wand and advised us that retiring was doable. At first, there was a lot of worry about whether we could manage for the rest of our life with what we had. Now, nine years later, we are still enjoying our freedom to do what we want when we want. We have managed to have some beautiful overseas and Australian holidays, and have spent money on improving our home. Kath has been a very important part in us being able to do these things due to the care taken to look after our portfolio. We look forward to being able to continue to work with Kath to follow a few more dreams in the future. Thank you, Kath, for all you have done to help us achieve our dreams. Your magic wand must indeed have superpowers!"

— B & L H (Mango Hill, QLD)

"One of the best decisions we have made was to entrust our financial management to Kath when we retired over 20 years ago. In those early years she was our rock and was only a phone call away whenever we needed reassurance as inexperienced investors watching the markets fluctuate. She encouraged us to enjoy our retirement and we have done very well with our investments with Goals & Dreams. We have become comfortable and confident investors under Kath's guidance and expertise."

— B & A F (Ferny Grove, QLD)

Attitude, Abundance & Action

I dedicate this book to my dear friend Jo,
who initially encouraged me to write it
and continues to provide ongoing love and support.

Attitude, Abundance & Action

How to create motivation,
mindset and magic around money

Kath Orman Dip FP, CFP

Attitude, Abundance & Action: How to create motivation, mindset and magic around money
Kath Orman

© Kath Orman 2024
www.goalsanddreams.com.au
aaa@goalsanddreams.com.au
PO Box 130, Chermside South. QLD. 4032.

This book is sold with the understanding that the author is not offering specific personal advice to the reader. The content of this book is provided as a guideline and is general advice only. For professional advice, seek the services of a suitable, qualified practitioner, who will provide tailored written advice, appropriate for your situation. The author disclaims any responsibility for liability, loss or risk, personal or otherwise, that happens as a consequence of the use and application of any of the contents of this book.

All rights reserved. This book may not be reproduced in whole or part, stored, posted on the internet or transmitted in any form or by any means, electronic, mechanical, photocopying, recording or other, without permission from the author of this book.

Editing, design and publishing support by
www.AuthorSupportServices.com

ISBN: 9781922375261 (pbk)
ISBN: 9781922375285 (e-book)

 A catalogue record for this book is available from the National Library of Australia

Acknowledgements

To my family, friends, clients and colleagues who urged me for years to write this book. The ideas, information and stories come from the entire melting pot of my journey so far. Thank you all for being on this journey with me.

Jo Ross, my dear friend. Thank you for being such a continued beacon of light, love and true friendship. My true angel friend.

Shelley Marshall, my beautiful daughter. Thank you for being my sounding board, for your ongoing love and support, and for proofreading when you had so many other things that needed your attention. You are such a blessing. Thank you for being such a wonderful mum to Iziah.

Bradley Marshall, my amazing son. Thank you for your cryptic comments and for always keeping me on my toes. I love your one-liners and quick wit. You keep me grounded.

Scott Charlton, my business coach, friend and mentor. Thank you, Scott, for always providing your sage and considered advice, guidance and support. Thank you for always being there for me and for your friendship and loyalty over many years.

Alex Fullerton, Louise Zedda-Sampson and Natasha Higgins at Author Support Services. Thank you for your patience and continued support in making this book the best it can be. You are very much appreciated.

It is with the greatest pleasure that I provide this foreword to *Attitude, Abundance & Action*, a wonderful and enriching book by Kath Orman. Within the pages that follow you will find the means to develop the mindset to live your best life, along with plenty of suggestions about how to put this into practice.

Looking back on our lengthy association, I think Kath was always destined to write this book. And we should all be grateful she did. When we first met the best part of 20 years ago, Kath was a highly qualified financial planner who was enthusiastic about empowering people to live their best life. Although her primary means was through astute financial management, I venture to say that it was Kath's passion for helping clients get on and enjoy life that created such a loyal following.

In all the time I have known Kath, her mission has not changed. She remains as passionate as ever about 'normal people' like you and me having the means and the confidence to get on and do the things we like to do. Blessed with a wonderful ability to demystify what is required to get on top of one's finances, Kath has been sagely guiding her clients through many major decisions such as house purchases, retirement, estate planning and, yes, having the trip of a lifetime. The hundreds of postcards she receives from clients enjoying themselves in all corners of the globe provide ample testimony to how effective she has been with this guidance.

So, what can you expect from reading Kath's book?

I expect you will find it very empowering.

Because she is a financial planner, Kath is well qualified to comment upon the fraught relationship between money and happiness. The latter half of this book contains good, sensible advice about managing your finances. Incorporating quotes from other extremely wise people adds to the richness of the advice shared.

But Kath's message has always been way more than what you would expect of a financial adviser. And so too you will find this book provides a very holistic message. As the title says, it's about attitude, abundance and action.

Happily, much of what Kath has to share you can implement for free, as early as today. That's because you don't have to wait until the end of the book. There's plenty to reflect and act upon within the first few pages… and it keeps on going after that. As she does in person, Kath has freely shared from her own experiences and provided lessons to be learnt from real-life scenarios.

I encourage you to read, reflect and savour the wisdom Kath has shared.

Scott Charlton MBA FCA
Director and Founder Slipstream Group
Coaching, and personal and business planning

Contents

Introduction	1
How to Use This Book	5

Part 1 – Attitude

Chapter 1	Are You Ready?	13
Chapter 2	Thoughts and Feelings	19
Chapter 3	Body Language	31
Chapter 4	Choices	41

Part 2 – Abundance

Chapter 5	What is Abundance?	55
Chapter 6	Wealth, Health and Emotional Wellbeing	65
Chapter 7	Move Over Clutter – Hello Abundance!	79
Chapter 8	The Key to Life is Balance	89

Part 3 – Action

Chapter 9	How to Create Your Wish List	105
Chapter 10	Explaining Financial Planning	123
Chapter 11	Where Are You Now?	129
Chapter 12	Knowledge – Face Your Fears	147
Chapter 13	More Investment Options	165
Chapter 14	Stories of Success	183
Chapter 15	Are You Excited? Act Now!	191

Find Out More	195
About the Author	197
Resources	199

Introduction

Congratulations! If you are holding this book in your hands and reading these words, you have begun the journey into making a difference in your own life. Something inside you has resonated with the title *Attitude, Abundance & Action* and you have purchased this book. You must feel ready to take a step forward in the direction of your dreams. Thank you for being brave enough to act on that feeling. The contents of this book may challenge the way you currently think (your attitudes), however, I believe the teacher arrives when the student is ready.

I have always had an inner knowing that one day I would write a book. I didn't know what it would be about. However, the universe, dear friends, family and clients have nudged, guided and strongly suggested that I should write it.

Since 1987 my main profession has been as a financial planner. I started my own business Goals & Dreams Financial Planning Pty Ltd in 2001. At the time, I was a single mum with children aged 10 and 6, with no other means of support. In hindsight, I wonder what I was thinking. As my underlying values were being suppressed where I was working, it meant that I had to have the courage to take a big leap into a very scary world of running my own business. I had to walk in my own truth. I truly believed that we should not just invest funds for people but care about them and their life and be with them on the journey. The structure in the corporate world did not have the same outlook, and it was all about writing the business and getting the money in the door.

It is many years later now and I am blessed with a wonderful client base of lovely people. It has been an absolute blessing to help them achieve their goals and dreams. I am passionate about helping people reignite their dreams. We get so caught up in the day to day 'drudge' of life that we often suppress that deep longing to enjoy the wonderful things life has to offer.

I was blessed to have grown up on a dairy farm at a wonderful place called Mt Pleasant, north of Brisbane in Queensland, Australia. The work was hard and the hours were long, yet I loved to be able to roam free in nature's beauty. One of the first films I ever saw as a child was *The Sound of Music*. I laugh now as I remember singing at the top of my lungs (while herding the cows). I would throw my arms wide and sing *the* song and run with abandon down the hills. Whenever I feel stressed and overwhelmed now, I close my eyes and recapture that feeling and energy of freedom. In recent years, I went to see *The Sound of Music* stage production in Brisbane with a lovely friend of mine, Maree. As I heard the orchestra play that song, my heart swelled with emotion and there I was back on that mountain again.

My dad always enjoyed a glass of beer or two and would say, "Katie is a financial planner because I drank beer." Apparently, I collected his bottle tops and could add and take away figures up to 100 before I went to school. Thanks, Dad. He also loved that song from Louis Armstrong, 'What a Wonderful World'. I immediately think of him whenever I hear it as the words are so special. Such a gift.

Several years ago, I was fortunate to meet an inspirational lady named Marylin (Maz) Schirmer, founder of the Un-Institute of Women™. She said that she was looking for people like me. I laughed and commented that I was rather busy running my financial planning business. However,

INTRODUCTION

I went on to undertake her training and became a facilitator, and was known as a Transformologist®, and have run workshops and retreats with another IOWI graduate. These powerful retreats were designed to help women release suppressed emotions and negative beliefs and start really enjoying life. As my financial planning business has continued to grow, I am no longer involved in this wonderful community, however, it has formed an integral part of my growth.

Through a wonderful connection made by a fellow graduate of IOWI, I was guided to attend a presentation by Don Tolman – The Wholefood Medicine Man. This was another blessing that has taken me on a path to understand how the body can heal itself using what nature provides to us in abundance and the wisdom of our ancestors. We are so blessed that his son Tyler is continuing to share this wisdom across the world.

I hadn't planned to wear as many hats as I now do, and for a long time, I did endeavour to compartmentalise the different things I do. Now they are all blended together, and it has made me into a more flexible and grounded human being.

I have also written poetry from a young age and now write a Christmas poem for my clients every year. It started in 2001 as a few stanzas and has now grown to two pages in a small font to fit it all in.

It is from this big melting pot that I draw knowledge from different areas to help you regain control and direction in all areas of your life.

There are many aspects, past experiences, thoughts and attitudes that have guided you to your current situation. If you want to make a change, the time to start is now. *Attitude, Abundance & Action* contains information based on my more than 35 years' experience as a financial planner to get you thinking and believing that you can achieve your goals and dreams.

As you read, I want you to feel that we are embarking on a journey together – one where you will have clarity and direction.

I may also challenge your past thinking to create new thought patterns and better habits and attitudes towards your future happiness.

The joy on my clients' faces as they share a wonderful life experience with me is the thing that keeps me passionate about what I do, and I hope that through this book I can bring joy to you too.

I feel so blessed to have this opportunity to write down these words to share with you, the reader. I will be so pleased if you feel grateful for the messages and learnings you gain from this book, and if they influence you (even in a small way) to make positive changes in your life.

Let's begin.

How to Use This Book

Have you ever said any of the following?

"I'm hopeless with money."

"No matter how hard I work or how much I earn, I never seem to get ahead."

"I don't know how to budget."

"I'm always scrambling to pay the bills from one payday to the next."

"My partner handles all the finances."

"I'll have to keep working until I'm 90 to have enough to retire."

"I'll never be able to travel the world."

"I'm so tired of just making ends meet."

"I'm just too busy and it's all too hard."

"Perhaps I'll get around to it one day."

"It seems others get lucky but not me."

If the answer is 'yes', the first step is to identify and become aware of your own negative talk. Take note when you hear yourself think or say any of the above (or your own mantra that you have been clinging to for years).

The simple fact of becoming aware will begin to change your attitude habit, and new thoughts such as *I now take ownership of my finances or I am attracting abundance to all areas of my life* will replace the old broken records.

Attitude, Abundance & Action demystifies the steps needed to allow you to be the driver on the road to financial freedom, while also enhancing other areas of your life in the process. You have an opportunity to realise how much abundance you already have and to understand how to attract more wonderful experiences, people and places into your life.

Financial planning is like a jigsaw puzzle. It can seem overwhelming when you first start, however, once you lay the foundations, it gets easier to fit the correct pieces into place.

This book will show you how we have all been influenced by our parents' attitudes towards money. As your knowledge and understanding grow, you will have little light bulb moments when you think to yourself, *Okay! Now that makes sense!*

Each part contains exercises and opportunities for self-reflection about your spending habits and your relationship with money. Remember that this is your life, and you are the one who can make a difference.

Some of the messages may be too overwhelming to take in at the beginning, and you may need to come back to them later. You may find as you progress and reflect that some of your answers even change! I do endeavour to write as if I were talking to you. You can imagine we are sitting together, sharing a coffee or a glass of wine, chatting about life.

I suggest you read through the whole book first and then reread it as these words are written in a sequence that will help you understand the whole process. There have been many times in my life when a book has inspired me to change my life, then much later I pick it up again, reread it and wonder, *How did I miss those other messages the first time around?* On reflection, I have realised it just means I hadn't been ready to see them earlier.

This book is filled with practical exercises. To get the most out of working with these exercises, I suggest you purchase a special journal with a beautiful cover (something that means a lot or jumps off the shelf at you). If the budget doesn't allow for that (yet) a simple exercise book will do. This special book can be used to work through the exercises and to take notes as you go.

This book will assist you to analyse all the separate compartments of your life and give you direction to ensure you are on the right path – just like the arrows on the tarmac at an airport show the planes the right path to take.

As the title suggests, *Attitude, Abundance & Action* addresses each part individually and then ties them all together in the final chapters. The third part, Action, is the largest as it puts everything you learn in the other two parts into practice.

Attitude

- Look at your preconceived ideas and how words that roll off your tongue or replay in your mind may be harmful to you.
- Become aware of how powerful negative self-talk can be.
- Be challenged to say enough is enough.
- Find out how to be willing to change and move forward with clarity of thought.

Abundance

- What does abundance mean to you?
- Many have found that when they have acquired the things they wanted, they didn't make them happy at all.
- Can you think of the last time someone came back from a wonderful 'life experience' holiday with a renewed energy and sparkle and wanted to share every detail with you? Did you want that to be you?
- What if you saw abundance in your life every day? The more you move forward to abundance the more the universe provides.

Action

- You are replacing the old worn-out thoughts with new ones.
- You are moving forward.
- You have considered what abundance means to you.
- It is time to act and apply practical measures.
- The power of writing things down cannot be underestimated. This is where the homework begins.
- Create a wish list. List your short-, medium- and long-term goals.
- Create a budget. How much do you need to live on?
- Your income: What do you earn?
- Your assets and liabilities: What do you own and what do you owe?
- What strategy will help you achieve the things on your wish list?

HOW TO USE THIS BOOK

- Build your knowledge about investing and take away the fear.
- Have fun! Remember to laugh and be excited – this is your life we are talking about.
- Learn from the experiences, achievements and challenges of other clients.

PART 1

Attitude

> "'The time has come,'
> the Walrus said."
>
> — Lewis Carroll

Are You Ready?

Did you know that everything we do in life is based on our past experiences, perceptions, influences and knowledge? They have guided us to where we are today. Some of those experiences may have been wonderful and have provided a fantastic grounding. Perhaps some of them haven't been the best and you want to change the direction of your future. Or perhaps the influences have been so subtle you are not even aware of the beliefs and attitudes you hold deep inside you. Some of these beliefs may be holding you back and getting in the way of living the life you imagined you would be when you were a child.

It can be a shock sometimes to wake up one morning and realise that we are 30, 40, 50, 60 or 70+ and we aren't where we expected we would be.

Sound familiar?

ATTITUDE

> **Be careful what you think because *you* are listening.**

Did you also know that the thoughts you think and the words you use determine your journey in life?

Be careful what you think because *you* are listening.

When you watch young children at play, you can't help but smile at how so full of life, joy and exuberance they are. However, so quickly they are directed to conform, sit still in a classroom, behave, don't do this, don't do that. That beautiful energy is zapped out of them and often creativity is squashed. They have visions of being a dancer, astronaut, firefighter or actor when they grow up. Depending upon their environment, they will either follow through with those dreams, change direction or simply give up and settle for less.

Often, this is because someone in their life commented, "You'll never be any good as a dancer/actor/doctor," and they believed them. Can you relate to this? Have you quashed your dreams and allowed the path of so-called normality to overtake your journey? I have seen this on many occasions and it is so sad. However, my plan is for you to read this entire book, be open and receptive to changing the way you think, reconnect with your dreams and live the life you REALLY want to.

"Too hard," you say? Well, that thinking is exactly what has got you to where you are right now!

Let's refer to the following checklist:

- ❏ My life is humming along perfectly.
- ❏ I am exactly where I thought I would be at this age.

- ❏ I have a wonderful relationship with my partner.
- ❏ I have a loving, supportive family.
- ❏ I have close friends who are there for me.
- ❏ I have a community network of like-minded souls who share the same passions as myself.
- ❏ I have a wonderfully fulfilling career.
- ❏ I am financially compensated for the work I do.
- ❏ I am living in line with my true values and beliefs.
- ❏ I find joy in every day.
- ❏ I always find something for which I am grateful.
- ❏ I am financially secure.
- ❏ I can travel wherever I want to in the world.
- ❏ I am fit and healthy.
- ❏ I love life.
- ❏ I enjoy every day, no matter what life throws at me.

Some of you may be blessed to have ticked all the boxes above; others may have some of these as goals. For me personally, life has handed me many lessons along the path. Sometimes I didn't get the message or take on board the learning the first time so I was sent another lesson.

However, now I am a little wiser, I choose to ask myself, "What is my lesson in this experience?" Life will always provide continued opportunities for growth. It doesn't mean that everything will always be perfect, it just means that when you have a handle on your 'attitude' you don't stay down for so long. You pick yourself up, dust yourself off, take a deep breath and solider on, ready to take on the world again.

ATTITUDE

EXERCISE

I am grateful for...

Pause and think of something for which you are grateful.

- On the first page of your journal, write down five to ten things for which you are grateful.

Leave a couple of pages blank, and as you think of other things later, add them to your list.

This exercise has a flow-on effect and will start to reframe your thought patterns and attitudes. It may seem rather magical when you see that the more you focus on the positive and feel gratitude for what you already have, the universe sends you more of the 'good stuff' of life.

It is easier than you think – you *can* do it! When I was growing up there was a sign in our lounge room: "I complained because I had no shoes, until I met a man who had no feet." While I did understand that message on some level as a child, it was not until later that I really knew the true meaning: there is always, *always*, something for which we can be grateful.

Often, just when things are starting to take shape, another challenge is sent to us. While I certainly wouldn't have selected some of my experiences from life's menu, they have shaped who I am today. In hindsight, often the biggest challenges bring the biggest blessings and reasons for change: new environments, new people and fresh energy.

Let your 'mess' be your 'message'. Often when you have a mess in your life, once you address the mess, you realise that there was an underlying message you needed to address and learn from.

> **"Let your 'mess' be your 'message'."**

"Watch your thoughts, they become words;
watch your words, they become actions;
watch your actions, they become habits;
watch your habits, they become character;
watch your character, for it becomes your destiny."

— Frank Outlaw

2

Thoughts and Feelings

We all have the little voices in our head that are constantly chattering away, usually with any number of opposing points of view. It is so easy to allow the force of the negative vibes to overpower the positive, and most of the time, we are blissfully unaware this is happening. The thoughts we think and the words we use set the framework for how we live our lives. When we become aware of these very human traits, we can begin to take ownership of the direction of the rest of our lives.

We often say terrible things to ourselves in our thoughts. A good filter is to ask yourself if you would ever say those things to a loved one or a friend. If the answer is 'no', then why are we saying them to ourselves? We deserve more love and respect... and a good time to start making this change is right now!

Let's consider reframing your thoughts. For those of you who think, *My life is terrible and I have nothing to be grateful for*, consider the following:

- Did you sleep in a bed with covers to keep you warm or a fan overhead to keep you cool?
- Did you have a meal to eat before you went to bed, and do you have food to eat for breakfast?
- Do you have running water to bathe in and fresh water to drink?

Waking up each day is a blessing. Some people go to bed at night and never wake up. Others leave their homes in the morning, never to return again due to unforeseen circumstances and life events.

> **Waking up each day is a blessing.**

What have you been thinking and telling yourself today? Did you bounce out of bed and automatically say, *This is a wonderful day and magic will happen*? I'm guessing probably not! It is more likely that as soon as you woke up your mind went to all the things that had to be done: iron clothes, put on the washing, make lunches, make the bed, pay the bills, blah blah blah. Am I correct? Yep? Well, one of my favourite sayings (yes, there are many) is "Today is the first day of the rest of your life."

Tomorrow, before you get out of bed, spare a few moments to think about things. Have a listen to outside noises. What are you hearing? Have you ever heard those birds before? Do you only hear traffic? If so, think how fortunate we are to live in a modern world where we can get from A to B in the comfort of a car, bus or train and fly in a plane that glides effortlessly through the sky!

THOUGHTS AND FEELINGS

It only takes a moment to change how we think.

I often imagine a little angel sitting on one shoulder and a little devil on the other. Of course, the angel is positive and uplifting and the devil is full of doom, gloom and negativity. I was acutely aware of these two when I decided to start my business.

As you can imagine, starting a business from scratch was a rather daunting task. I left a well-paid position that ensured my mortgage would be paid and went to a self-employed position where nothing was guaranteed. I was a single mum with two small children so that regular income was a security blanket. There was quite a dialogue going on in my mind: *What makes you think you can run a successful business?* said the little devil. To which the angel replied, *Of course you can do it, as you know in your heart the way it is meant to be done. You KNOW you can do it!*

EXERCISE

Morning self-talk

For the next seven days, write down the thoughts that enter your head when you first wake up each morning.

Then review your notes at the end of the week.

- Were you aware of your own thoughts and self-talk?
- Are you in a bit of a rut with negative thoughts running around your mind?

Repeat this exercise the following week.

- Have your thoughts changed?

The choice about what you think is yours alone.

Yesterday morning when I woke up, it was raining. Instead of feeling down, I thought how the lovely rain will help my garden grow and save me time having to water it.

It is powerful when we realise that we cannot change what happened yesterday. We only have power over how we let the past impact today. We can choose to let go of whatever happened yesterday and face the new day with strength, courage and a sense of expectation that wonderful things will happen. While we plan and dream about tomorrow, today is the only day we have that we can be part of NOW.

EXERCISE
I love me!

I have been an avid fan of the beautiful Louise Hay for many years and have been fortunate enough to meet her on a couple of occasions. As some of you may know, Louise was a big fan of mirror work. It takes a lot of courage to bounce out of bed in the morning and look at yourself in the mirror and talk to yourself nicely. Try it tomorrow morning.

- Look right into your own eyes and say "I love you!" (And mean it!)

This may sound crazy, however, it is extremely powerful. How can your partner, family or friends love you if you don't love yourself?

Doing this exercise helps us to understand how our thoughts about ourselves impact on everything we do every day. If we are kind and gentle to ourselves and genuinely believe we deserve to live a happy and fulfilled life, we will start to attract these things.

It can take a bit of practice to master managing your thoughts. How long have you been telling yourself negative things? Remember that your brain is like a computer and registers whatever information you send it.

If you are 40 and have been feeding your subconscious negative information about yourself since you were a teenager – say aged 14 – it means that for 26 years (365 days x 26 = 9,490 days, not counting leap years), you have been reaffirming things like "I'm too fat/tall/short/young/old/stupid/shy to get anywhere in life." The brain registers this input and then goes about fulfilling this and providing circumstances which prove your words to be correct.

You can change that, you know.

Can you imagine how powerful it is when you change your data feed? I am a very tall woman and have been 5' 10" (178cm) since I was 11 years old. In fact, I had to carry my birth certificate with me to prove I was a child and not have to pay an adult entry fee. I towered over all the other kids, even the boys. As children can be rather cruel, I was teased a lot. Part of me wanted to shrink down and pretend that I was shorter. When we would go to the local dance, a boy would ask me to dance and I would get up... and up... and up... and his face would fall as he realised how tall I was. I hated walking into a room as people would automatically check out how high my shoes were. My negative self-talk and thoughts were undermining my self-confidence. It bothered me then but it doesn't anymore.

> **❝ You can change that, you know. ❞**

Fortunately, my parents always encouraged me to walk tall and be proud. When I was on a school camp to the Snowy Mountains at age 13, someone took a photo of me posing beside a snowman. Many years later, people guessed my age from that photo and someone thought I was 28. It still makes me laugh when people do a double take, and realise I am that tall. In reality, there are many women who are much taller than I.

When we take the time to stop and think and become aware of what we allow ourselves to dwell on, change happens. For some, it may be a slow realisation that the influences we have been programmed with since childhood have had a huge impact on our lives. For others, it is like a light bulb is switched on and the world is now viewed through very different eyes.

Figure 1. Kath at the Snowy Mountains age 13

Our environment, family, friends, teachers, etcetera, have a huge influence on our perception of ourselves. Some of this may be wonderfully positive and some of it may not. These influences can be passed down from generation to generation, with the feeling of low self-esteem held deeply within our cellular structure. However, we are now in a time of enlightenment and self-empowerment. We all have the ability to make a difference, not only to our own life but to others' lives as well. Awareness and attitude are very powerful tools.

Think for a moment how you feel when a dear friend or family member starts berating themselves and putting themselves down. You can see what a wonderful person they are and you believe in them. You talk to them with love, kindness and encouragement because you believe in them. It's true, isn't it?

You would never talk to that same friend with the same words, thoughts and adjectives as you tell yourself, would you? Yet, you can look into the mirror and think awful things about yourself. Isn't it time to be gentle and loving with yourself?

I had a co-worker once announce that she always gets sick at Christmas. She was quite astounded when I said, "Of course you do." When I explained that because she has been telling herself that for so long, as soon as the subconscious hears Christmas carols and sees Santa everywhere, a switch is flicked. "Okay," says the brain. "It must be time to get sick." Does this sound familiar?

EXERCISE
Making it happen

Write down three things you do well.

They could be being a good friend, a good cook or a good listener. You may be great at time management, parenting or being a good daughter, son or workmate. You may be really good at arts and crafts.

Write down the last time you were proud of yourself.

It may have been because of something you created, said, believed in and saw through to fruition.

We seldom allow ourselves to do this, do we?

Love yourself. It is powerful. Our thoughts are powerful and the energy we put out attracts like.

THOUGHTS AND FEELINGS

EXERCISE
What are you thinking and feeling?

When you start looking into your thoughts, their origins can stretch back many years.

- What thoughts from the past are still running through your subconscious?
- Are those thoughts or beliefs still true?
- Were they ever true, or were they just someone's perception of you that you adopted at a young age, believing it was true?
- Are they relevant to your life now?
- What new thoughts that are positive and nurturing to your soul can you replace them with?

This can be a challenging exercise to do at first. Allow things to come up and don't think about them too much before you write them down.

How often do we help a friend who is going through troubled times, and how often do we give them a hug? Why not mentally or even physically give yourself a great big, fat, warm and loving hug right now.

I read somewhere recently that one of the best things to count in a day is how many hugs you have either given or received. The number they suggested was five for great emotional health. Now, I have always been a hugger. I love to give and receive hugs. However, as I live on my own for two weeks of every month, I wondered how was I going to give or receive five hugs per day. As soon as I became more conscious of this, I realised how many hugs I *do* receive from friends, clients and family members. This awareness created many of those hugs. I have a beautiful vibrant client who is 93 years young and sometimes calls into the office just to receive hugs from all our team – one each when she arrives and another when she leaves. She is an inspiration to us all.

Many years ago, I was an elected trustee of a major bank's Staff Superannuation Fund. At the time I was 28. The very first meeting was held in a big ivory tower in Sydney with a security guard at the door. My self-talk ran something like this: *What am I doing here? I'm just a kid from a dairy farm in the bush! I'm the only woman, and there is Sir... and other highflyers!*

I took a deep breath, stood tall and walked in to take my spot. About five minutes into the meeting I realised that the people around the table were there for their business acumen or other reasons. I too was there for a reason. I had grassroots knowledge of the impact of the decisions that were about to be made. I found my voice and spoke up, contributing to the discussions.

The chairperson thanked me for my valuable input, and I learnt a great life lesson. If I had sat there timidly without speaking up, the change that needed to be made would not have happened. All the members of the fund who relied on me to be their voice would not have benefited from the changes that were implemented as a result of the meeting.

Your thoughts are not just annoying, bothersome things – your thoughts help shape your actions and your reality.

THOUGHTS AND FEELINGS

When I started my business in 2001, I was told that I wouldn't have any clients because nobody would trust a woman as a financial planner. For a little while, I allowed those words to wash over me, but self-doubt tried to overtake. However, I am a Taurus (the bull) and those comments were like a red flag. I remember thinking, *Just you watch me! I have two babies to provide for with no other support! Failure was not an option. I could have allowed that thought to take hold and shape my reality, but I'm glad I didn't.*

> **Your thoughts help shape your actions and your reality.**

There were times over the years, however, that I thought back to that comment and wondered if it was valid. What was I thinking to take this on? However, I believed in myself and I had to walk in my own truth and values. I now feel blessed to have built a loyal client base with beautiful people and feel proud that I have made a difference to their lives as they have to mine.

"The human body is the best picture of the human soul."

— Ludwig Wittgenstein

Body Language

Have you ever taken the time to stop and watch the people around you? It can be an amazing revelation. There is so much you can tell about a person by observing how they walk, their facial expressions and their general demeanour.

Do you realise how much *you* give away about yourself by the way you hold your body, your expression and the way you walk? These things all show the world how you are feeling on the inside. We all have days where we just want to curl up and run away from everything, as is a natural human reaction in times of stress. It is beneficial at such times to take a deep breath, stand tall, pull your shoulders back and go forth into the world instead! It may sound a little melodramatic but it works!

Growing up on a dairy farm, surrounded by peace and tranquillity, it was a rather daunting experience when I was introduced to my first crowd as a small child. I remember feeling so excited about going to the Brisbane Exhibition (The Ekka) and then feeling overwhelmed looking at kneecap after kneecap in a sea of bodies. I had never seen so many people in one place before. Even though I'm older, taller and wiser, all these years later, I still find myself taking lots of deep breaths when I am faced with a sea of people.

I have always been a keen observer of people. Over the years I have come to realise how unhappy most people look as they go about their daily journey. They rush here and there and just look so sad. I've also found that in cities where it is cold, there is seldom any colour in their clothing, especially in winter. I am from Brisbane in Queensland, where we have beautiful sunshine and enjoy a subtropical climate. We tend to wear brighter colours. I love to visit Melbourne where there are wonderful cafes and restaurants, however, there are so many people wrapped in their dark colours, heads down, making their way about their business.

> **You will never see rainbows if you are always looking down.**

Now and then I will catch someone's eye who must be thinking the same thing as I am, and we share a knowing smile.

I was driving to work one day recently, and it was a rainy morning. I passed a bus stop with about a dozen or so passengers huddled together, all looking down at their phones. Only a few minutes later, the sun came out and the most beautiful rainbow appeared. I don't know about you, but I have always loved the magic of a rainbow. It's nature's beautiful gift. It was on that day that I came up with the phrase "You will never see rainbows if you are always looking down." It was only later that I found out Charlie Chaplin had said something similar!

A fun thing I have done with my children since they were small is to watch people – especially at airports. I would ask my children to become aware of someone walking past and tell me what they can tell about this person. With the wonderful perception children have, they would say, "Mummy, look – here comes a happy lady," or "Mummy, he looks so sad. Should I give him one of my smiles?" As they grew older, they became more attuned and comments would be, "He looks like he has had a sad life and has given up," or "I bet that lady laughs a lot."

The art of picking up body language is diminishing as many people these days are often too busy staring at their phones to even be aware of their surroundings let alone be people watching. Remember to look up and see the clouds, rainbows and beautiful nature.

I remember a particular man from many years ago because he made quite the impression on me. He walked so confidently and his smile was so welcoming. He had me at hello and we ended up going on to date. Although we did not end up as life partners, we are still friends after all these years. I still love to watch him walk whenever we catch up for a coffee or a glass of wine. The way you walk can be so sexy. It is the self-assurance and confidence that is attractive. I'm not talking an egotistical swagger like in Rod Stewart's song 'Da Ya Think I'm Sexy?' – although, that can be fun in the right environment… chuckle, chuckle.

Now, guys, I know you like to watch women walk in a sexy way and I've done some research on this (talked to guys). It is funny how their initial reaction is to just laugh and agree. "Of course I love to watch women walk," they'd say. When I questioned them about what was attractive, they stopped and thought about it. An example I provided was if Elle McPherson walked into the room, then everyone stops. She is a stunningly beautiful woman who carries herself so well. She has a beautiful energy and is known as 'The Body'.

ATTITUDE

> "I speak two languages,
> Body and English."
>
> — Mae West

Unanimously, every male I asked came to the same conclusion: if a woman looks happy, confident and easy to get on with, they are more likely to want to talk to them. This book isn't about dating, however, we are all energetic beings and the energy we give out either repels or attracts others.

I have also had lots of interesting encounters as a woman when meeting a man in a business context. Most men are polite and shake my hand with respect. Some feel they have to crush my hand as a power play. One time, a man who was in a successful role but much shorter than me, almost pulled me over with his attempt to retain power while he shook my hand.

I recall a time many years ago when I was first starting out in my career. Prior to becoming a financial planner, I had a boss who suggested that I would be a good financial planner and should undertake further studies. Many years later when he retired, he and his wife became clients. He was really planning ahead!

One of my first tasks as a financial planner was to ring banking clients and talk to them about a possible upcoming legislation that may impact their business. I felt so nervous and insecure, and my stomach was filled with dragons, not butterflies. I remember walking in each day, sitting down at the phone and making the calls. Some 20 years later, I ran into a lady who worked in the same office at the time. She said to me that she always remembered how confident I seemed and how calm I was as I spoke to the clients. What? You've got to be kidding me! I was so blown away by her feedback, as that is definitely not how I was feeling at that time. I was a nervous wreck. However, I must have been able to walk in confidently, put on a brave facade, keep my thoughts positive, sit up straight and just get on with it. Fake it until you make it!

With age and experience comes wisdom. I now love interacting with people as I know I can help them because I care.

Watching others can teach you a lot about yourself. When people watching, another simple filter is to ask the following question: Is the person operating from a position of love or fear? You can usually tell the choices people have made in their life by what is shown on their face. When you see someone who is world-weary and looks like they never smile or find much joy in their life, they have probably been fearful of life's journey. On the flip side, when you see someone who radiates happiness and joy, they have probably made a different choice. We are all subject to challenges in our life, yet if you let what happened in the past overshadow today, you are giving away the ability to embrace the love of life and will be stuck in fear.

> **"Watching others can teach you a lot about yourself."**

If I am about to walk into a room, I take a moment to consider if I am happy to be there or fearful. If the answer is fearful, I then ask myself why. There is a very strong link between the way we think and how these thoughts flow into our body language. It is just about being more aware and questioning those feelings and not letting negative self-talk win.

When I learnt about this, I was amazed how easy it made life. It helped me understand the human element and even understand my own reactions to situations. When we are worried or anxious it is usually because we are fearful of what might happen. We draw towards us all the possible negative outcomes that may eventuate. The fact that we focus on the fear often draws it towards us via the Law of Attraction. It isn't easy when we are faced with overwhelming situations, yet if we begin to train ourselves to visualise a positive outcome and hold those thoughts, we are more likely to attract a better outcome.

I'm sure we all know people who are so caught up in fear and worry that they forget to see any other possibility or solution.

I met this lovely, quiet lady while I was helping run a retreat designed for women (nothing to do with financial planning), and towards the end of the retreat, she quietly asked if she and her husband could come to see me for financial planning. He was due to retire in ten weeks and was concerned about the future.

I remember the first meeting so well. We met at my office and immediately I could see the fear in her husband's eyes and body. He would not meet my eye and was nervous, coming from an obvious position of fear. We talked through their situation, and I was able to assure them that all would be fine and life in retirement held all the things that were on their wish list. To cut a long story short, after working through their wish lists and financial situation, we prepared the written recommendations for their retirement. At their third appointment, he was a different man completely. He was looking forward to the future and was so much more relaxed. In fact, at the end of that meeting, he gave me a hug! He retired on 4 July that year and the next week they took off on a trip to Tasmania and I was so happy to receive their postcard. I have recently met with them for their annual review, and he commented that he is so chilled with everything now that he has been retired for 9 years and enjoying the journey.

ATTITUDE

> ### EXERCISE
> ## *Love or fear*
>
>
>
> Next time you walk into a crowded room, ask yourself, *Am I happy or fearful?*
>
> - When you are able to, note your reactions in your journal.
> - If you were fearful, what caused you to feel that way?
>
> This exercise will help you find a new layer of insight and a different way of looking at life. When you understand this for yourself, it certainly makes it easier to understand and process how others are feeling. Sometimes, we may not be able to take away their fear, however, we can be there for them, providing support and love through the process.

Our body language and the way we hold ourselves when we walk tell the world so much. I am sure we have all had the experience when someone walks into a room and we feel it immediately. Some people emanate such negativity that it makes everyone instantly feel uncomfortable. On the other end of the scale, some people enter a room and bring a lovely flow of energy and exuberance. These are the people you gravitate towards and want to be around. Others just creep into a room hoping to go unnoticed.

When I was younger, I hated walking into a room because I was so tall. However, I now walk in proudly with my head held high, with an expectation and the thought, *I wonder what wonderful people I will meet at this gathering?* Which person are you? Next time you look in the mirror, look at how you are standing. Are you standing tall or are your shoulders drooping or hunched? What expression are you wearing?

Remember, a smile costs nothing yet it can make such a big difference, not only to how we feel in ourselves, but how we are perceived by others. Which person do you want to be in the future? It is never ever too late to make a change.

Just last week I was faced with a number of challenges, and I gave myself a strong talking to. I said to myself, "Get up, walk tall, show up and never give up!"

> **Get up, walk tall, show up and never give up!**

"Life is what happens when you
are busy making other plans."

— John Lennon

4

Choices

Now you have begun to question your thinking and body language, it is time to move on to what you can choose to do in life. I am sure most people would agree that it would be a blissful life to always be happy without troubles, cares or worries.

Life has a way of often handing us unexpected challenges and situations that we would prefer not to experience. Most people react in a "Why me? Why now? What have I done to deserve this?" mode. But some people seem to take it all in their stride. Why is this? If you view challenges with a positive attitude and learn from the experience, it helps you grow and develop. You will become wiser and often turn the negative into a positive. In fact, the people who do this are often grateful for the opportunity to make changes that will take their life in a different direction.

Often, the cosmos/universe/divine has a plan for us that we are unaware of. What seems like the worst blow in the world can often be the launch pad to wonderful new experiences and events. Opportunities, people and situations can present themselves in unexpected ways and life takes a totally different path. How often has something happened in your life that you had not planned for and you can now look back on it with gratitude as your life has been enriched because of the challenge?

I have so many clients who had their position made redundant and they come into my office feeling sad and emotional, obviously worried about being able to pay the bills and support their family or themselves. I explain that I understand how they are feeling and empathise. From the financial planning perspective, I suggest that we pick up the emotion, put it in a big bubble over to the side and talk practical issues. It is very hard to make big decisions when we cloud the situation with lots of emotion. I know because I am a rather emotional creature. I do have a very logical and practical side though. My head and heart often have a tug of war. Then my intuition kicks in and I go with the 'knowing' feeling.

In these instances, we work through their actual situation, and I ask many questions about their life and if there is a path they haven't taken but always wanted to. Have they had a dream to open their own restaurant, undertake further studies or change career completely? This wake-up call often reveals a deep, suppressed dream or goal. Alternatively, if they are happy in their chosen career, often a much better position with less stress and sometimes more money comes along.

When things look like they are financially falling apart, I encourage people to think of something that is positive in the situation by using the word "Fortunately..." and then filling in the blanks.

For example:

- *Fortunately,* I have good health.
- *Fortunately,* I have time to consider options.
- *Fortunately,* I have the opportunity to take a break.
- *Fortunately,* I have cash at call to live on.
- *Fortunately,* I have friends and family who are supportive.
- *Fortunately,* I am resilient.
- *Fortunately,* I am able to slow down for a little while and rest.

Being able to change your mindset from 'woe is me' to looking at your blessings can be your saving grace. This attitude change is like flexing a muscle. The more we train ourselves to have a different point of view and see things with a different filter, the more natural it becomes as part of our make-up. Every day, choices become easier and the natural Law of Attraction provides more like-minded people, events and situations.

Whenever I am faced with big 'stuff', I look to my benchmark of previous challenges. The absolute worst day of my life was the day I almost lost my daughter, Shelley, to meningococcal meningitis at the age of seven. This is when I truly learnt several lessons. The first lesson was to go with my gut feelings. Shelley was not feeling well, and I took her to an after-hours doctor. They were rather dismissive and sent me home. To be fair, she had a sore tummy, a fever and was lethargic. I was up all night with her while she was unwell and vomiting, which often happens with children. However, something inside of me felt there was more to it.

Listening to my mother's intuition, we took her to our own doctor the next morning. They called an ambulance straight away and she was raced to hospital. To cut a long story short, it is a horrible thing that takes over very quickly and we nearly lost her in the ambulance. In the emergency ward, it came down to five-to-ten-minute intervals: if she lives through these five minutes... then ten minutes... It was every parent's worst nightmare. Fortunately, she survived with no loss of limbs and is now a successful professional dancer, actor and choreographer. Over the years I have felt so blessed to see her on stage, with those beautiful long legs that she could have lost, not to mention her precious life. I still get goosebumps when I talk about this.

That is my benchmark, and no challenge (and I've had a few) has ever come near that awful experience and for this I am truly grateful. I also have a very healthy appreciation for health and wellbeing and have been blessed on this journey to have learnt more about how the body is able to heal itself.

Sometimes, life just becomes so overwhelming and it is easier to choose to drown in the experience. It overwhelms us and we get stuck in a pit of negativity. Why does this happen? It is because we are human. When we realise that we *do* have a choice and can make changes that *will* impact our lives, we can work towards solutions and more positive outcomes.

EXERCISE

What do you want?

For some of us, our limiting beliefs and suppressed emotions are holding us back.

It's time to write a new script for your life! The next page of your life can either hold wonderful promises of love and happiness or can be a carbon copy of the previous page, repeatedly more of the same.

What do you want from life? Stop telling yourself what you *don't* want and start telling yourself what you *do* want!

🌿 Write down ten things you want in your life.

When you have written your list, is there one thing that you could implement now as a step towards something on it?

I was at a presentation many years ago where the presenter drew a diagram showing a stick figure in a pit. I resonated with this because when you are feeling down, you feel stuck. I have drawn this little pit for many people over the years and they automatically nod their head with understanding. However, the secret is to understand that we should only allow ourselves to be in the pit for a short while. Don't move in with the couch and the TV and plan to stay there.

Figure 2.1. Pit of Misery

Figure 2.2. Don't stay in the pit

I have found that when I allow myself to feel my negative emotions, it helps me acknowledge and allow those feelings to be worked through. I put a time limit on how long I will allow myself to be in the pit. After a period of wallowing time, I'm often out of the pit before the end of the time limit as I don't like being there. I take the time spent in there to acknowledge the situation and then work out possible solutions and options. There is something quite powerful in giving yourself permission to be sad. For example: "Okay, today I will allow myself to feel the human emotion of sadness." By lunchtime you may feel that you have had enough of feeling that way and you want to get on with the rest of your day.

Depending on what the driver is, you may need longer than a day, as certainly there are many overwhelming circumstances in life that take longer to heal. The loss of a loved one, divorce or illness can be crippling.

There is often a ladder to climb out of the pit, and you can get out and see the sun shining and hear the birds singing, and you are able to realise that life goes on. Sometimes we forget the ladder, which could be in the shape of a friend, colleague, support group or family member. Perhaps just talking to another human being can be all we need. If your situation is more serious, then there are many professional avenues of advice to pursue.

ATTITUDE

EXERCISE

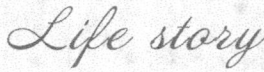 

Life story

This is a big exercise. Allow yourself at least an hour to complete it. Also leave several pages in your journal afterwards should you wish to add more notes later. Don't worry about how your story comes out – it can be in dot points or prose or even poetry. The main thing is to write it.

- Sit down and write a story about your life.
- Write it all down and leave nothing out.
- Pour out how you feel and what has happened.
- Is there a little person inside you who was deeply hurt or influenced as a child, which has impacted your adult life?

Remember to include the happy moments as well as the challenging ones. When you review what you have written, what does your writing say about how you felt?

- Did you feel like a victim or are you proud of how you overcame the problems?
- What else do your words convey?
- Do you want to be this person, or do you want to lift yourself up and move forward in life with determination and a resolve to make changes to live the life you imagined?

This exercise is all about getting to know yourself a little better so that, as you move forward, you can possibly make different choices.

The language that runs around in our heads either keeps us stuck or lifts us up.

A very simple change to how we view our situation can be by reframing our negative sentences by adding 'in the past'. One of my clients in her early 30s came to see me. Almost the first words out of her mouth were "I'm hopeless with money" and proceeded to tell me all the things that she did not want. I guided her to amend her original sentence to: *"In the past, I have been hopeless with money."*

> **The language that runs around in our heads either keeps us stuck or lifts us up.**

I paused and asked her what she *did* want. She looked a little stunned and had to think about it. She has spent so much time channelling all her energy into what she didn't want and didn't have that she was stuck. She eventually shared that she wanted to feel empowered and in control of her financial situation. She wanted to do the things on her wish list and to feel like she was getting somewhere in life. She then shared that saying those words made her feel so much better, and we hadn't even started working on her financial situation! Might I share that she is now a proud home owner, takes holidays (and sends postcards) and has a nest egg set aside as well as a growing superannuation balance for the future.

The more you put energy into what you don't want, the more you receive of the same. Think about it. When we say to our children, "Don't run on the road," where does your mind automatically take you? Our mind works in pictures, so the child automatically visualises running on the road. If I were to say, "Don't think about a pink elephant in a tutu," you might immediately start thinking something like, "How cute does that elephant look?"

It is best to say to our children, "Take care when you cross the road." They then visualise being careful. Words and images are so powerful, and your brain cannot separate the negative from the positive. When we say things like "I'm always late," the brain accepts this as the norm and (without you consciously knowing) makes things happen so you are late, just as it believes you want. If you don't believe me, just try it for a week or two and see if anything changes.

Can you see how incredibly *powerful* it is to be mindful of your thoughts and words?

My involvement with the Un-Institute of Women™ has been so life-changing for me. It has taught me a lot about myself. I feel blessed to have met Marylin (Maz) Schirmer many years ago. Maz has developed a simple and very gentle process called Creatrix®, which is specially designed to deal with the female brain to release the inherited emotions and beliefs via epigenetics. Many of us have deep suppressed emotions and beliefs that are not only ours but have been passed down from generation to generation and are embedded in our cellular structure.

At the time we met, I was certain that I had no time in my already busy life to undergo training with Maz. However, I knew it was something I had to do and, somehow, I made it happen.

One of my core values is to make a difference in the world and I did think that was just through financial planning. However, the universe keeps sending me situations and beautiful people who have provided further learning and skills, which help me to help others.

Often, the very things we seek in life are being blocked by our own limiting beliefs and suppressed emotions. We don't feel good enough at some level to receive the abundance we crave. Sometimes we are even aware on a conscious level that it is our own doing. More often, blocks lie at a deep unconscious level. It's that preprogrammed feeling that whatever we do, we never get ahead, achieve or get to experience the things we want to in life.

It is so liberating when we rid ourselves of those feelings. It brings pure joy to see people emerge from the cocoon and spread their wings and fly. Often these emotions put lines on our faces and make us look older. I have seen the impact that releasing these emotions can have. One lady at a retreat truly looked ten years younger in just a week. It was such a shock when we looked at her before and after video. She is now empowered and taking ownership of the direction of her life and the choices she makes, as well as helping other women. Look out world!

PART 2

Abundance

"Happiness is a choice, not a result. Nothing will make you happy until you choose to be happy. No person will make you happy unless you decide to be happy. Your happiness will not come to you. It can only come from you."

— Ralph Marston

What is Abundance?

I am sure that the first response most people would give when asked the question, "What does abundance mean to you?" is "An abundance of money!" As a financial planner, I have assisted many people achieve abundance over the years. One of my favourite sayings is a quote by Leo Rosten: "Money doesn't buy happiness, but neither can poverty."

However, there are so many things in life that provide an opportunity to experience abundance and they don't cost a penny. As we progress through the book, we will tie all the parts together and help you on the path to financial freedom and empowerment.

Isn't 'abundance' such a beautiful word?

Abundance!

> "The situation in which there is more than enough of something."
> — Cambridge Dictionary

> "A very large quantity of something."
> — Oxford Dictionary

> "The number of atoms of one isotope of an element divided by the total number of atoms in a mixture of the isotopes."
> — Dictionary.com

In Latin, the word *'abundantia'* means 'overflow'.

Not all of us can see the abundance that already exists in our life, especially when our focus is usually on what we don't have.

We are so blessed in this modern world to have a plethora of modern appliances to make our workload lighter. We have a washing machine that washes our clothes, a dishwasher for our dishes, pots and pans, a vacuum cleaner, hair dryer and electric razor – the list goes on.

> ❝ Not all of us can see the abundance that already exists in our life. ❞

It is so easy to forget the things that we *do* have as we focus so much on what we *don't* have. We leap out of bed, have a shower, grab some breakfast, race out the door and jump into our modern car, equipped with air-conditioning, music and a GPS to make sure you don't get lost. We have Bluetooth to be able to talk as we drive along or play music via our modern phone. It comes to us so easily now that we don't even think about it.

We drive to the airport, board a plane and in an hour or two we are in another part of Australia. In other parts of the world, we can be in an entirely different country in that short space of time.

Cast your mind back to the not-too-distant past when, if you wanted to travel somewhere in a hurry, you had to get out of bed and either saddle up a horse to ride or harness the buggy to the horse or team of horses. The pace of life was much slower and often the work much harder. I'm not saying we don't work hard now. Unfortunately, I believe that we are all endeavouring to fit so much into every day that we forget what is really important!

As I write these words today, it would have been my grandmother's 122nd birthday if she were still alive. She passed away at 93, so she did have a long life. I often think of the changes our grandparents have seen in their lifespan. The pace of life is getting faster and faster as we scurry around like hamsters on the ever-spinning wheel. Yet, we often take for granted the many changes that have been made over the years, which were meant to create an abundance of time.

The ability of human beings to continue to innovate and create is mind-blowing. Anything to do with computer technology is almost obsolete before it is released, as there is always the promise of something bigger, smaller, better, faster and more amazingly wonderful that is designed to bring happiness to your life. But... does it really?

What really makes us happy? I have spent much of my life on the hamster wheel, endeavouring to be the perfect mother (superwoman), wife, partner, employee, business owner and friend, and it can be exhausting.

We strive for perfection, yet somehow it continues to elude us. When we stop and take a deep breath and appreciate the wonderful world we live in and the people around us, it is so refreshing.

Hopefully, we have family and friends who love and appreciate us, and we can nurture them in return. If you have toxic people in your life, take stock and gently remove yourself from the situation. As we are all energetic beings, when our energy is good and pure we attract like-minded people and situations.

I have found the more I am in tune with who I am and walk in my own truth, the more I attract beautiful people who are on the same wavelength. It doesn't mean I don't empathise with someone who chooses to always play the victim as I will always help someone in need. I have also spent a lot of my life being a 'rescuer'. However, I have learnt that unless someone is willing to make a change, take a stance and be the change they want to see, my help, guidance and assistance is wasted. In fact, the universe sent me situations several times before I got this lesson!

I took a short break from my business to allow the creative juices to flow and to finish writing this book. They say if you write a page a day, in 365 days you will have a book. It may work for some, however, I found that after dealing with people's lives and numbers all day, I didn't feel very creative at 9.00 pm at night. During my writing break, I stayed on a beautiful mountain with magnificent views, surrounded by nature's abundance. The moment I walked in and put my bags down, I felt re-energised. Tony O'Connor's soothing music was playing and a little fountain was running. All over the place, there were candles burning and vases filled with gorgeous roses. How welcome did I feel? (Thank you, Joy and Tony). In fact, I hadn't realised how tired I was until I stopped.

WHAT IS ABUNDANCE?

Can you relate to this? Where I stayed there was an abundance of sunshine, blue skies, amazing sunsets and birdlife. The kookaburras greeted me each morning, laughing away in the trees nearby, and I watched the brightly coloured parrots flying from tree to tree. I had beautiful music playing in the background, and I enjoyed long walks in the rainforest. It was so good for the soul.

I went away to finish writing this book, however, the unexpected bonus was that it helped me to practise what I preach: to slow down and appreciate the abundance of the world around me. To stop and smell the roses.

At home, I walk my dog each morning. I am fortunate to live near cows and horses in paddocks and ducks on a pond. I do appreciate the sunrise each morning and feel a bit lost if I must forgo my walk due to early business meetings or appointments. I feel particularly blessed on those mornings I see a koala sleeping in a eucalyptus tree.

Perhaps you did not expect these words from a financial planner. Maybe you thought I would just be focusing on the dollars! Well, of course the dollars are important. Having financial freedom provides so many more choices in life. Most people say they would be much happier if they had more money. I can certainly relate to this and understand. Yet, I have seen time and time again where people who believe money will make them happy are still sad when they get it, as the quote at the beginning of this chapter implies.

A tale of two winners:

1. A couple won $750,000 in the lotto. They were already good at budgeting and managing money. They sought professional

advice, made their money grow, enjoyed life and had more choices available.

2. About the same time, another couple from the same town won $500,000. A year later, they made the front page of the newspaper as they had purchased 19 cars for friends and family and were back living on welfare benefits.

The Psychology of Money, a book by Michael Argyle, tells us that at a very deep level some people do not believe they deserve money, so they do everything they can to get rid of it. The second couple above is a case in point. It is likely that they weren't really doing this at a conscious level – it just happened as they didn't know any better. They believed at a very deep subconscious level that they didn't deserve the money, so their self-talk actually created the result.

Can you see how we think and feel plays a huge part in our relationship with money? Well, not just with money but everything we do in life? What is your self-talk regarding wealth? Have you had the situation (or situations) in your life where, just when you feel you are getting somewhere, something happens and the money slips through your fingers?

I saw my parents struggle through years of hardship on the farm. We had many years of devastating drought: tanks ran dry and the creeks dried up. We watched cows die and it was so very sad. To support the dairy farm we grew pineapples and other crops, and I remember Dad being so excited about an amazing crop of huge watermelons that were due to be picked. The semitrailer was due to collect them the next day, but nature had other plans and a huge hailstorm demolished the whole crop. The result became cow feed and the expected income was lost. Living on the land and in nature is wonderful, yet it can be so challenging. I wouldn't trade how I grew up for anything in the world. While the work was hard, there was a wonderful sense of community, songs shared around the campfire, dancing at the local dance hall and lots of fun to be had.

Yet, watching my parents struggle made me vow to be good with money and learn how to budget and have a reliable source of income. It always helped me realise how people's attitudes towards money can be deep-seated and their beliefs are often passed on without them being aware. How often in life do we hear our mother or father's words come out of our mouths? We all do it. Our parents can pass on wonderful wisdom and sound advice, and sometimes they are passing on what they learnt from their parents, generation after generation. All too often, the legacy is one of fear and lack and instils a subconscious belief that they don't deserve wealth.

> **Empowering ourselves with increased knowledge and understanding creates a new energy.**

Empowering ourselves with increased knowledge and understanding creates a new energy. You are then ready to attract the abundance you desire. The cycle of the past can be broken.

I love this affirmation from Louise Hay: "I am open and receptive to an abundance of health, wealth, love and happiness in my life and I accept it now!"

ABUNDANCE

> **EXERCISE**
>
> *Abundance*
>
> Ask yourself the following questions. Write everything down as it comes into your mind. Don't curtail – let it flow.
>
> - What does abundance mean to me?
> - What in my life do I feel is abundant?
>
> When you have answered these questions, leave some room then finish the following statement:
>
> - I would like to enjoy enriched abundance in the following areas…
>
> Leave a page after you complete this exercise so that if you come back to it later, you can add other things.

Now you are developing a much clearer picture of where you are and where you want to be. I am getting excited for you! Each piece of the journey is important and will provide better results if you are truly honest with yourself and you do indeed *want* to make a difference.

EXERCISE

Moving forward

Write down the things that you say to yourself that undermine your situation, for example:

"I'm hopeless with money/relationships/my health choices..."

Now change the sentence to begin with "In the past", for example:

"In the past, I was hopeless with money/relationships/my health choices..."

You can also try this affirmation:

"I now take ownership of my choices and decisions and will continue to take on new learning to remove any fears (known or unknown) about accepting abundance in my life now!"

"Miracles start to happen when you give as much energy to your dreams as you do to your fears."

— Richard Wilkins

Wealth, Health and Emotional Wellbeing

The happiest people I have ever met live each day enjoying all that life has to offer. There are many elements that contribute to this outlook.

Wealth

In dealing with my clients over the years, I have seen so many situations where clients are very wealthy (from a financial point of view) yet they are not happy in themselves. On the flip side, I have seen clients who initially may not have financial wealth yet they are happy in themselves and radiate a positive attitude. These people are generally ready to take on new learnings to make a difference in their financial life.

It is when people decide that they want to grow and develop as individuals and experience all that life has to offer that the change begins to take shape. It often arrives as a light bulb moment when my clients realise that their attitudes and beliefs about many things in their life have a flow-on effect to their current situation and relationship with money. On some level, they may not believe that they are entitled to the peace of mind and security that comes with taking ownership of their financial situation and other areas of their life. Once they take ownership of the direction of their life's path and become empowered, it provides not only a sense of calm but also a sense of direction and control.

We are all human and sometimes have doubts and fears about many aspects of our lives. When I ask questions that perhaps they haven't considered before (about what really matters to them in their life, not just their personal financial wealth), it opens a doorway to a new way of thinking and new possibilities.

The topics I might ask them to consider are:

- taking the trip of a lifetime
- the birth of a child or grandchild
- purchasing their dream home
- being able to retire early
- pursuing their dream job
- establishing their own business
- being philanthropic
- obtaining a clean bill of health after an illness
- losing weight and undertaking an exercise program
- meeting their soul mate

- hosting the much dreamed about perfect wedding
- orienteering around the world, which helps them stay fit and healthy.

EXERCISE

Wealth

Write a list of five things wealth means to you.

Health

I'm sure everyone reading this book has attended a sad funeral. While funerals are always sad, it is even worse when the person was too young and passed away far too early from an illness or an accident. Life happens. It is a wake-up call for those who are left grieving.

It is at times like this we often think about our own mortality and our health.

I have always hated taking any sort of medication. During a difficult time in my life, I developed a thyroid problem and was given tablets to take. I hated it even though the doctor said if I didn't take them, I would die! Pretty strong words. Of course, these words create fear.

During this time, I learnt more about energy healing and the emotional connection to my illness. My voice and opinions weren't being heard in my relationship at the time, and I was suppressing my emotions and feelings. And guess where the thyroid is located? In the throat! This contributed to the thyroid problem, therefore I needed to heal the whole situation, not just the outcome. In addition, the throat chakra is all about communication.

I learnt a lot about my health from Don Tolman and his son Tyler. Don's wisdom comes from a lifetime of research into how, in ancient times, our ancestors were more in tune with nature and how the body is able to heal itself, given the right environment.

When I first heard Don speak, the underlying truth of his words resonated with me. I got goosebumps. I was brave enough to change my eating habits and increase my intake of mushrooms and pineapple (nature's gift for thyroid problems), and I was able to stop taking the medication. (Note that this is not a recommendation for you to do the same without further research.) I have always had a healthy diet, so it was easy for me to adopt Don's 7 Principles of Health into my life. I have also chosen to become a vegetarian. In fact, about four years before meeting Don, I listened to my body and reduced my intake of red meat. I have never felt healthier or happier, and I've been told I looked ten years younger after changing my diet. Finally, after all those years I look younger instead of being told I looked 28 when I was only 13!

> **Many of us know what we need to do – we just aren't doing it!**

Our health is so important. Many of us know what we need to do – we just aren't doing it! I believe so much in what Don Tolman teaches about food and health that I have now become a 'ringleader' and happily assist as a crew member for both Don and Tyler when they visit Australia and hold presentations, workshops and advanced learning.

Don Tolman's teachings subscribe to the theory that if we learn to listen to our body, it has the potential to heal itself within three to seven days, given the right environment of rest and nurturing and using what nature provides. For more deep-seated illnesses, we also need to investigate if there is an emotion being suppressed that is causing the illness. Just treating the result is only temporary; we need to find the cause.

Below is a short summary of the 7 Principles of Health that have assisted me.

The 7 Principles of Health

1. Air

Wind clears the air of toxins. If you are working in an office or inside all day, you need to be getting outside at least five minutes of every hour to get some fresh air. You can also try sleeping with a window open so the air can move around in your room.

We don't always breathe properly. Our subconscious breathing just happens. When we are not taking deep breaths, we often feel frazzled and overwhelmed. Whenever you are feeling this way, go outside and take deep breaths.

If you can, go outside, sit quietly somewhere and do this breathing exercise: Breath in deeply for seven counts, hold for seven counts and exhale for seven counts. Pause for seven counts before inhaling again. Repeating this simple exercise just seven times can restore balance to both mind and body. Even better if you can do this at the beach or in a beautiful rainforest.

2. Water

Water is the gift of life.

We need to drink at least two litres of water a day just to keep our brains hydrated. For every 22 kilos you weigh, you need to be drinking a litre of water to keep your body happy and eliminate toxins. It is important that it is clean, filtered water, not just liquids that contain water. Quite often a headache can disappear just by drinking water.

3. Sunshine

Sunshine is our natural emotion lifter as it heals the cells in our body.

If you feel depressed and walk out into the fresh air and sunshine, you automatically feel your spirits lift and you feel better.

In Australia we have become afraid of the sun. Many of the sunscreens we use have toxic chemicals in them and create more problems. It may cost a little extra, however, it is worth seeking out more natural remedies. Depending upon your skin type, gradually increasing your exposure to the sun – starting with, say, ten minutes – is a wonderful way to get your vitamin D naturally. I have found that since I have improved my diet and removed toxins from my body and environment, my skin hardly ever burns anymore. Of course, I still have a healthy respect for the sun and use common sense.

4. Walking

If you spend a lot of time sitting, find a way to get out and about and go for a walk.

Try walking for 30–45 minutes in the open air (not on a treadmill).

On some cold and chilly mornings, I feel like rolling over and staying in bed. However, then I think about how good I feel when I'm in the fresh air. It sets me up for a much better day than just jumping out of bed and rushing. Make it part of your lifestyle at whatever time of day you can – somehow you can fit it in.

The benefits of this simple exercise are so powerful. It impacts on your health, emotions and overall state of wellbeing. Especially if you become more aware of your environment and nature when you are out walking. My dog certainly loves it.

5. Wholefoods

Did you know that nature has provided us with an abundance of foods that are specifically designed to aid and heal certain areas of our bodies? By way of example, walnuts, broccoli and cauliflower are shaped like the brain and are good for the brain. Tomatoes and capsicum have four chambers, are red and are good for the heart. Any plant leaf that has a lot of veins is good for our blood supply. Avocados are shaped like the womb, take nine months from seed to fruit, and are good for women's reproductive organs. The list goes on and on.

How did I get to this age and not realise the connection – and I grew up on a farm? The more we increase our intake of natural, chemical-free foods, our bodies will just love us. We then become more attuned to listening when our bodies talk to us.

Next time you are in a supermarket and you reach for an item, turn it over and read the contents. Is it filled with numbers (chemicals) or is it real food?

If you are overweight, often you are eating foods that have low or no nutrients. Your body then tells your brain that there was no nutrient in that so give me something else. Then the vicious cycle of binge eating starts. When I make nutrient-rich CABALA juice (Carrots, Apples, Beetroot, Lemon), quick as a flash I can feel it zooming around my body providing energy.

6. Non-toxic relationships

Some people are a joy to be around and others are not. We may laugh at this, however, the impact of toxic people in our life can be huge. It can impact on both your physical and mental health.

Once you remove yourself (or limit contact) with toxic people, you will begin to attract more loving people with beautiful energy to your life.

It may be easier said than done, but awareness is the first step.

When you no longer choose to deal with their demands and issues, you realise what a drain it was. No more walking on eggshells.

7. Passion

What are you passionate about? What gets your blood pumping and excites you? Okay, we all need *that* sort of passion in our life – the human touch, the passion of sex between loving couples that certainly gets the blood pumping – and it is good for our health!

Yet, what are you passionate about in your working life? Are you following your chosen path or just turning up to get paid? Sometimes it is hard to be in tune with our innermost desires to do, be, make, create or assist. Often the very schools and world of academia that are meant to teach and educate us squash our natural exuberance. The word 'passion' can be viewed as the 'passing of ions', which means we get ions of pleasure from doing things that we love.

It is so important to find out what you love doing and follow this path.

EXERCISE

How healthy are you?

Review the 7 Principles of Health and write down the things you would like to be doing that you are currently not doing.

Emotional wellbeing

A grateful heart is one of the biggest learnings I can share. When we start to love and appreciate what we already have, we become a magnet for attracting more wonderful things, people and events into our lives. Changing our mindset is a conscious choice.

> **EXERCISE**
> *What makes you happy?*
>
> List ten things that make you happy.
>
> Depending how stuck you are in the 'woe is me' syndrome, it will either be a challenge or you will begin to see the benefits.
>
> Being happy then starts to become part of your DNA. Your awareness increases and you find yourself noticing things that you had previously been oblivious to. I promise you, it feels good.

During my workshops, many people have initially commented that they have nothing to be grateful for. Really? Think again. It all depends upon your filter and mindset. People sometimes sit there with their arms crossed and feel so strongly that their life is worse than everyone in the room. Perhaps it may be. Or perhaps everyone has faced a number of challenges and chosen a way to get through by enjoying each day, no matter what is happening.

Abraham Lincoln said, "Most folks are as happy as they make up their minds to be," and it's true. When I'm faced with challenges, I have often reflected on a point in time where I should have been more grateful. Then a new situation comes along and, in hindsight, where I was before seemed so much easier yet I didn't see it at the time. I am sure we can all relate to something happening in our lives that has caused us stress. Then we hear a story that is so sad, we realise that our own troubles are minor in the big scheme of things.

Feeling loved

We all long to be loved. We want to have a happy home that is filled with love and laughter.

For those who are parents, the way we love our children is beyond description. Once they are placed in our arms at birth, our life changes forever. I was not aware of the depth of emotion attached to holding my own child until I became a mother. When Shelley was born, I was so excited that I didn't sleep for the first 48 hours. I remember the first time I went out into the world pushing a pram. I kept thinking "I'm a mother! I'm a mother!"

Being a parent is one of the most challenging yet rewarding things you can do. When I was pregnant with my second child, Bradley, I kept wondering how I could possibly love this child as much as the first one. However, of course you do. We have this endless capacity in our hearts to spread our love further and further. If I had been blessed to have six children, there would still be so much love for each and every one.

Now I am a nanna, I have found another new layer of love that I didn't know existed. My little grandson Iziah fills my heart with so much love, joy and happiness. It is the circle of life.

There is no doubt that we have a large capacity to love our family, partners and friends. However, how much do we love ourselves? This is really the bottom line.

> **EXERCISE**
> *Who do you love?*
>
> Write a list of all the people in your life who you love.
>
> Write another list of all the things in your life that you love.
>
> When you have finished, review it. Did you include yourself?

How can we expect to attract the perfect partner or mate if we don't love ourselves first? It took me a long time to learn this. I have always been a people pleaser and (in the past) have gone out of my way to help others and be there for them. Yet, for many years, I didn't hold myself in such a high regard. It is wonderfully enriching when you come to terms with who you are, warts and all. To love the body we are given and who we truly are is such a gift. Of course, we can always be a better person and the journey starts by loving ourselves.

How often do you treat yourself to something special? It doesn't have to be big – a nice candle, a bunch of flowers, a pretty scarf, some delicious dark chocolate (perhaps not too much!). You buy such things as gifts for others, but what about for you?

One of my dear friends (darling angel Jo) and I have a pact. We buy ourselves a bunch of flowers each fortnight and send a photo to each other. It is like we are each receiving another bunch as well. We don't need to spend a lot of money yet the joy it brings is amazing.

Loving relationships

One of the biggest lessons I have learnt is to surround yourself with people who uplift you instead of dragging you down. We all have experience with these types of people. Some play the victim and, if we allow it, can suck the energy from us like a vampire. They leave feeling better for having spent time with you, however, you are left drained and depleted.

When we are around people who lift us up, we become energised and feel so much happier. We look forward to spending time with these people and want to be around them. We have found our tribe.

Just take a moment to think how you react when your phone rings and you see the caller's name. How do you feel? Is it a feeling of joy or do you have to take a deep breath and not want to answer the call?

If you can, remove toxic people from your life or, at least, reduce the amount of time you spend around them. I often imagine myself in a pink bubble of protective light if these types of people are around. My bubble protects me from their negative energy, and it is my choice how I let them impact my world.

"Get rid of clutter and you may find it was blocking the door you've been looking for."

— Katrina Mayer

7

Move Over Clutter – Hello Abundance!

We all lead such busy lives, and what can tend to happen because of this is that we accumulate clutter all around us. When I grew up on the dairy farm, nothing was ever thrown away because it may be recycled and used for something else. I can still hear my dad saying, "I've got something to fix that, Katie," and he would disappear into the barn. However, most of us don't have huge sheds, barns or other storage areas to store all our stuff. Having grown up in this environment, I have tended to be a hoarder... (in the past!)

Louise Hay wrote about decluttering and it really resonated with me, so I started to clear the clutter in my home and the office. The message I learnt from her writing was that if you have cupboards bursting with stuff, you are telling the universe that you don't need any more! Cleaning out your wardrobe, for example, makes way for

ABUNDANCE

new clothes or makes you realise that you don't really need as many clothes as you have. We tend not to wear many of the things in our wardrobe and just stick to our favourite items. Marie Kondo, who is an organising consultant, also has a range of books and even a television show, which provide wonderful advice. Marie applies a filter when decluttering and asks the question "Does it bring you joy?" If the answer is no, then it is either thrown out or given away.

I have also learnt that the clutter we have around us represents the clutter in our brain. I can relate to that.

EXERCISE
Clutter clearing

What does your work environment look like? Is it surrounded by piles of papers and files, all vying for your attention? When I become overwhelmed with my financial planning workload, I take all the files into another room, place them on the table and then sort through them and place them in order of priority. I feel so much more in control and organised when I have sorted through my Tower of Terror! I write down what must be done and then begin the tasks.

Now it's time for you to do the same.

- What areas of your life and environment need to be decluttered?
- What can you do to declutter them?

If you are having trouble with some items, apply Mario Kondo's question: "Does it bring you joy?"

Stephen Covey's book *The Seven Habits of Highly Effective People* also has a companion kit of several audio tapes. I found the information very useful in helping me to manage my tasks. At a recent training day with my staff, I was looking for a quick way to summarise his wisdom. There is now a YouTube clip that runs for 6–7 minutes and summarises the book. Refer to the Resources chapter in this book for further details. It is worth looking into, as it helps sort through what is both important and urgent, not just important. Some days everything seems both important and urgent, but one only has so much time.

> **The clutter we have around us represents the clutter in our brain.**

Setting decluttering goals

I have lived in my current home for many years now and it is time for a change. Gradually, I have been working through decluttering, sorting, fixing, painting and general repairs. It is a big task. I recently organised a six cubic metre skip bin to be delivered over a long weekend and in no time at all it was full. So much stuff! There were also several trips to drop off donations to various charities. It was exhausting yet so exhilarating when it was done.

You must be in a determined mood to declutter. Remember the reasons why you are doing it: to get your life sorted and simplified. Being a very sentimental person, it can be challenging when you find things that the kids made when they were little.

> **You must be in a determined mood to declutter.**

A few questions that worked for me:

Clothes/shoes

- How long since I wore this?
- Does it still fit (it's a great feeling when it is now too big – woohoo!)
- Do I absolutely love it?
- Does it bring me joy?
- Do I feel wonderful when I wear this?
- Would this suit someone else?
- If I put in back in the drawer or on the hanger, will I wear it in the next month?

Cupboards/memorabilia

- How long since I used this?
- Did I realise I still had this?
- Does it bring me joy?
- Is it just gathering dust?
- Could someone else benefit from this?
- Would I like to give this away and replace it with something that reflects who I am now?

Paperwork/files

- Do I need to keep this anymore? (Always check how long you need to keep important legal and taxation documents).

In this wonderful age, we can now scan paperwork and store it on our computer. If you do, make sure you back up your data. One way of doing this is to pay your bill, scan it and shred the original – that is, if you don't already receive your bill online. You will find this so liberating and there will be space on your desk in your home office (if you have one).

Of course, there will always be the situation where the original paperwork is required, like a birth certificate or similar. As I drown in paperwork every day in my business, it is refreshing when I can reduce the amount I need to retain at home.

When I really get stuck into the job, I am amazed at how determined I can be. You can sort your things into four categories:

1. Give away or recycle
2. Throw away
3. Keep
4. Sell (which can increase a savings goal).

Tip: Do not have a 'think about it' pile! Try to handle items only once and decide at the time.

Decluttering also makes you more cautious of bringing home items from the shops. Do you really need another ornament? Yes, it may be cute, but will it just gather dust? You can then decide if you want to admire it and put it back or buy it. Or you may find something that you absolutely love and now there is room for it in your home because you got rid of all the old stuff.

Quite often, when we surround ourselves with stuff, we are trying to find happiness in things, perhaps even because there is something lacking in our lives. However, there are some things that just resonate with us on a deep level and there are things that have a meaning and deserve a place in our hearts and on our shelves.

While writing this book, I found a gorgeous glass-blown, pyramid-shaped paperweight. The centre has swirls of blues and purples and it spoke to me. It wasn't expensive yet sits on top of my papers as a talisman for completing this book. It does bring me joy when I look at it.

At one stage we were in a particularly busy time at work and needed extra assistance with filing and archiving. We were fortunate enough to be blessed with a young lady named Phoebe (who is a dear friend of my daughter) who loves filing and turning the chaos of large files into order. She had some spare time in her busy schedule and came to help us sort out our files. In the process she cleared out our pending drawers, which were filled with sundry files and bits and pieces relating to people with whom we had a first meeting but they did not continue or did not fit the type of client we were looking for. Within a week of clearing these drawers, the phone was running hot with referrals. They came from our lovely clients who were sending us other lovely people – in fact, the perfect people with whom we wanted to work. In a short time, we had 17 new clients.

> **"** Quite often, when we surround ourselves with stuff, we are trying to find happiness in things. **"**

This was a perfect example of clearing out the old to make room for the new.

We set aside a whole day each year to give the whole office a spring clean and declutter. As the years go by, we are finding that we don't need the whole day as the team is becoming more ruthless each time.

When my son Brad was much younger, he and my daughter were clearing the table after a meal one night. In his wisdom, he asked me "Mum, do I throw this away now or put it in the fridge and throw it away next week?" I had to laugh. How many containers do we keep in our fridge with the intention to use the contents? Then something else is put in front of it and it is forgotten until we clean out the fridge. Does this sound familiar?

> **❝ Never underestimate the energy of clearing your home, office, space, heart, schedule and so on ready to receive abundance. ❞**

Never underestimate the energy of clearing your home, office, space, heart, schedule and so on ready to receive abundance. The clearing makes way for new energy, opportunities and situations.

Manifestation

I have always believed that we attract what we think about, drawing to us either positivity or negativity.

An example of this was when I had been in Sydney for a few days of financial planning training. My accommodation was close to Circular Quay (at Sydney Harbour). Each day I would look out the window and it was another rainy day. On the Saturday, I planned to check out of my accommodation and hop on the train to visit a friend at Hornsby. When I woke that Saturday morning, it was a simply stunning, beautiful, fine and sunny day. Now, if you have been to Sydney, you will know how beautiful the harbour is, especially when the sun reflects off the sparkling water like diamonds, and the Opera House stands there so majestically. It's quite a sight.

I decided to go for a long walk around the harbour, have a coffee and then collect my bag and board the train. After the walk, I took a moment and stood back, taking it all in, taking deep breaths and thinking to myself how grateful I was and how happy I was within myself. What a journey it had been to get to that point. After the negative things that had happened in my life, I finally felt peaceful and content.

I then thought of my dad and the song he loved by Louis Armstrong 'What a Wonderful World'. The words of the song floated through my mind, and I was enjoying the moment. A little thought then crept in, *Wouldn't it be nice to have someone to share this with?*

Honestly, within two minutes, a man walked up to me and commented on my height and asked me to join him for a coffee. I had been single for several years and been so busy with everything, I hadn't been on so much as a date, and here was a man in the middle of the day asking me for a coffee. Well, of course I said yes. It turned out that we had a lot in common and we became good friends and had a magical time together over the coming months, travelling between Brisbane and Sydney and even sharing a trip to Adelaide.

In later conversations, he said to me that he had no idea why he walked up to me that day, as it wasn't something he would normally do. He was on his way to pick up his daughter yet stopped to talk to me and have a coffee. He laughed when I told him (not on that first day) that I had manifested him!

> "Today is the first day of
> the rest of your life."
>
> — Charles Dederich

8

The Key to Life is Balance

Time. Wouldn't we all love an abundance of time? We are each given the same amount of time each day as everyone else on the planet, yet we each use it differently. When you add it all up, we all have a total of 10,080 minutes each week. Over the years, I have found that the best way to make use of time is to live in the moment instead of somewhere in the future or past.

In the past, I have been guilty of channelling too much energy into one area of my life at the expense of another. Now I have learnt to be present wherever I am and enjoy the experience. If I am at the beach with my kids, that is where I am. If I'm at the office

> **The best way to make use of time is to live in the moment.**

working on a project, that is where my headspace is. Of course, being a woman, I still think about what I'll make for dinner or what washing needs to be done at some point in the day. Balancing our busy lives is a challenge and often at the end of the day, we feel depleted of energy and wonder what we have achieved.

There is that fine line between procrastination and enjoying the moment. When I am working on a project, I become very focused on the tasks that need to be done, with the end result clearly visualised. Over time, I have become much more adept at prioritising, not just for making time for tasks but being more open and receptive to creating space for fun times as well. It is quite liberating when we let our inner child out to play. I have spent much of my life being responsible and taking ownership and getting the job done. When you do this, it is so easy to procrastinate and put other things off for another day. I'm sure many of us are guilty of that at times.

> **There is that fine line between procrastination and enjoying the moment.**

I have found, though, that taking a break to go for a walk outside and enjoying the fresh air and sunshine makes me so much more productive in the long run. You come back to the task with renewed energy and focus and usually sail through whatever must be done much faster, because you have nurtured your soul's yearning to be outside in nature.

EXERCISE

Work/life balance

Consider the following:

- What does your work-life balance look like right now?
- Is it balanced?
- How would you like it to be?

Once you have made a list of what you would like the balance to be, write down what you can do now to start working towards a more balanced day, week, month and life.

My daughter is a performer and a few years ago she was performing in a show at the Brisbane Powerhouse. I went to see her performance several times (of course, being the proud mum). I recall very clearly organising to meet a dear family friend there before the show on a Wednesday night.

My friend and I sat on the deck, overlooking the Brisbane River with a glass of wine, chatting and watching the sunset. So beautiful. I remember thinking, *Look at all these people out and about enjoying life on a Wednesday night.* It was certainly better than going home to do the washing and clean out the fridge. The show itself was amazing and we had a fabulous time.

Now, I knew those jobs still needed to be done eventually, yet that night really impacted on my thought process of how I spend my time. It is so easy to fall in a heap at the end of the day and think I'm too tired to do anything. However, if we keep doing this, life will just pass us by. I am fortunate in that respect now that my children are older. It has snuck up on me and comes as a surprise that I no longer have the hectic schedule of ferrying my daughter to dancing and my son to football and other parent-related duties. What goes around comes around, and now both my son and daughter often volunteer to be the driver if I want to have a glass of wine or two at a party. Aren't I lucky?

> **If you are still in a hectic time of life, make a vow to yourself to enjoy it.**

If you are still in a hectic time of life, make a vow to yourself to enjoy it. Talk to the kids on the drive. Play games. Sing songs. Be present with them and don't stay in the headspace of what is happening at work. One of the best questions to get them thinking is to ask, "What is the best thing that happened to you today?" It resets their thoughts to focus on something positive instead of tales of woe that someone pulled their hair or pushed ahead in a line... you know the rest (if you have kids).

Those words have come back to me now my kids are adults, and they ask me the same question. It makes me laugh.

When was the last time you put on your favourite music and danced around the lounge room? Do you find time to meditate and calm your busy mind? I find that when I am clearer, I am more receptive to either accepting invitations or organising get-togethers with friends and family, and there is more balance in my life, sprinkled with love, laughter and happy times. Precious moments are created that become precious memories. Each time I have followed through with an invitation from people I want to spend time with, even though I may be tired, I feel so much better having a laugh and enjoying the occasion. On the flip side, it is also wonderful to come home, cook a nice meal, wind down and just be.

EXERCISE

There are so many beautiful guided meditations to choose from. Meditation helps us to slow down and get our headspace where it needs to be.

Several years ago, I purchased a set of *Take Ten* CDs for my staff to listen to in a quiet office and just escape for ten minutes. Now there are a plethora of options available via Spotify or downloads. Both your body and mind will thank you if you meditate.

You may be saying that your mind is too active and continues to think a zillion thoughts at once. Like going to the gym, meditation takes practice. It is worth the effort.

- Purchase or download a guided meditation and try it out. You can find meditations and relaxations to follow on apps on your phone.

If you meditate already, try to create a regular routine. If you have a routine already, well done!

I have done my fair share of working long hours, studying, juggling and more juggling. It can be exhausting. If you are a single mum or dad, you will understand.

I recall a client meeting many years ago. A very busy man and his wife came to see me. He was an executive and was looking to move from one state to another. He didn't have a lot of time for our appointment and wanted all the answers without giving me time to ask the questions. During our discussions, I endeavoured to include his wife in the discussions. She sat there with her arms crossed, looking sad and did not say a word. He asked whether they should rent or buy when they moved. I asked how he felt about having to move. He was rather abrupt and stated that he didn't think that was a financial planning question. I responded that this is their life and I am just trying to seek an understanding of their situation. Finally, the wife spoke up, "Well, Kath, my whole world has been turned upside down. We have four kids, one child in the last year of high school, two at university and another at primary school, and it is breaking my heart to have to move so far away." The words and her feelings just continued to pour out.

> **" The words and her feelings just continued to pour out. "**

The husband looked gobsmacked. He had been so busy and focused on the business side of the move, he hadn't considered his wife's feelings. There had not been an open and honest discussion between them. To his credit, he looked straight at her and said, "I didn't know you felt like that. We need to talk."

They went off with the homework I had given them, even though he thought he earned too much money to do a budget! When they arrived for their next appointment, they came in holding hands and seemed so much more on the same page with smiles on their faces.

I see many clients with similar stories all the time.

We all need to be careful that we don't get so caught up in the daily hullabaloo of life and the constant pressures from everywhere and forget our loved ones who really matter to us.

EXERCISE

How often...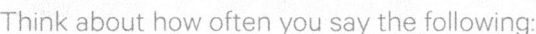

Think about how often you say the following:

- I love you.
- I appreciate you.
- Thank you for doing the washing.
- Thank you for taking out the garbage.
- Thank you for...

Also think about:

- How many hugs you gave today.
- How many hugs you received today.

They say to be healthy we need to give and receive five hugs each day. Do you have some catching up to do?

One simple rule: practise what makes you feel good. I have a friend who has several brightly coloured t-shirts emblazoned with FREE HUGS across his chest. You guessed it – he gives and receives many free hugs, and I am sure on many occasions, it makes the day of both the giver and the receiver. Giving and receiving a hug releases oxytocin (the cuddle hormone) which makes us feel all warm and fuzzy. Oxytocin is a neuropeptide, which promotes feelings of devotion, trust and bonding. The hormones released after a hug also assist in lowering blood pressure. Hugging also reduces feelings of loneliness and reduces stress. Pretty powerful, aren't they? Bring on the hugs is all I can say!!

> **What music do you listen to when you are driving to or from work?**

What music do you listen to when you are driving to or from work? Do you listen to music you enjoy, or listen to the news and get caught up on all the gloom and doom in the world? Depending upon how you are feeling, you could put on a relaxing piece, or if you need something loud and upbeat, go with that instead! Sing along! It doesn't matter if your voice isn't the best; it will make you feel better.

EXERCISE
Making time

We can have all the time for other things but not for ourselves.

Think about something you would really like to do for you. Write it down. Also write down:

- What you would do if you had an extra 5, 10, 30 minutes (or more) each day.
- What you would need to change for this thing to happen.

Do you need to do everything yourself? Can you ask for help and share the load?

Your needs could be as simple as wanting 10 or 20 minutes to be alone, have a bath, enjoy a cup of tea or to have a coffee in peace. When my kids were little, the idea of having a bath without being interrupted was like a dream – lying back in the bubbles with nice music playing and a candle burning. Such bliss, with nobody screaming, "Mum, where are my blue shoes?" or "Have you seen my football?" or "Where is my school hat?"

When I actually set the boundaries to say that Mummy needs some time just to be by herself (when the kids were old enough to understand) they took it on board quite easily and saw it as a challenge to leave me alone (and find their own shoes, hat or football).

I sometimes wonder if our mothers realised the environment they created for us, with the push that began in the 1960s for women to have it all. Now, many of us have wonderful careers, juggle the kids and the running of the household and endeavour to spend time with our partner to keep the romance alive. Yes, we have it all – but gee it can be tiring, and I often hear the words "What about me?" Women fall easily into the category of trying to be a superwoman and trying to be everything to everyone. Put up your hand if this is you! (Me too – in the past – well maybe still a little bit now!) However, there are many single dads who also fall into this category as well and we give a big cheer for the hard work you are doing too.

> **❝ Women fall easily into the category of trying to be a superwoman and trying to be everything to everyone. ❞**

Do we really have to do it all on our own though? Is there someone who could help? How much do you value your time? Think about what your hourly rate is and see if you can work it into the budget to pay someone to help with some of the household chores. If you are more likely to clean the house before the cleaner comes, stop it! If the windows need washing, there are local people desperate for work via Air Tasker.

The time you spend with your children or partner is so much more important than having the cleanest windows or a pristine home. Even if you are on your own and have a busy life, go and see a movie or do something for you! I treasure the memories of time spent with my kids walking along the beach, building sandcastles, and playing hide and seek. It also helps us let our inner child out of the adult body. Make time for the special people in your life. Organise a date night, and take a weekend break at the beach or in a cabin in the mountains. Talk to each other, and share and dream together. Make time to catch up with friends and family you may not have seen for a while. Please do this instead of only seeing people at a funeral.

> **"** Talk to each other, and share and dream together. Make time to catch up with friends and family you may not have seen for a while. **"**

Many of us get so caught up in providing for our families that we forget to experience the joy of everyday experiences with our family and friends, a beautiful sunset, a piece of music or a beautiful flower.

ABUNDANCE

EXERCISE
Write a list

Do you feel guilty that there never seems to be enough time to do all the things you want to do? Are your thoughts overwhelming and all-encompassing?

If you are still struggling to find time write a list of everything you need to do.

This will provide clarity and direction. Make it a habit to write things down instead of keeping them on your mind. A list won't reduce the number of tasks; it just helps give a little peace of mind. The action of taking the things out of your cluttered mind provides order. You can then prioritise and sort the order of importance and work through the tasks with more direction.

I have a lovely framed poster in my office. It shows an elephant with his trunk up (which means good luck) at the beach, balancing on a beach ball. Whenever I feel stressed and overwhelmed, I use my elephant to help get my feet back on the ground.

Figure 3. Elephant balancing

PART 3

Action

> "Once you choose hope,
> anything is possible."
>
> — Christopher Reeve

How to Create Your Wish List

This is the exciting part of the process: the one where I encourage my clients to write their wish list. Now it is your turn! This list will include your short-, medium- and long-term goals. I suggest you really delve deep and consider all the things that have been rattling around in your head for so long but may have never actually been verbalised or written down.

Even though the next exercise lists separate areas of your life, they all affect your overall wellbeing and are connected.

Now we're going to jump straight into things.

EXERCISE

Reality check

Copy this chart into your journal. Feel free to add or remove any areas so this list is relevant to you.

You can also download this chart from www.goalsanddreams.com.au.

Consider the nine areas of your life that are listed. Refer to the heading in each column and ask yourself the question in relation to each area of life. Rate each section from 1 to 10, with 1 equalling a little and 10 equalling a lot.

Areas of life	How fulfilled are you?	How much of this do you feel you deserve?	How grateful do you feel?
1. Money			
2. Happiness			
3. Health			
4. Love			
5. Spirituality			
6. Family			
7. Hobbies and fun			
8. Career and success			
9. Friendship			

Once you have written your answers, make notes in your journal about your observations.

1. Money

Most of us would like to make improvements in this area. In my experience, there is little time spent in our schooling that addresses financial literacy. We may learn complicated mathematical calculations, but we don't learn how to live on a budget, avoid massive credit card debt and plan for the future. This means we are raised with little to no understanding of how to manage our own personal finances unless our parents teach us. Many of our parents have no idea about this either, and thus the cycle is perpetuated generation after generation.

This book offers many tools and a great deal of information, but sometimes we need someone to help us a little further. If you find you are feeling overwhelmed, you can work with a financial planner. Finding one whom you trust and feel comfortable with may be the step you need towards finding financial freedom.

I feel blessed to enjoy a very special relationship with my clients. I make sure that they have a sound understanding of what we are doing and that they have ownership of the decisions made. They must be able to sleep at night and not be worried. That applies for me as their financial planner as well.

When looking for a planner, make sure you can communicate with them and that they don't use jargon or talk down to you. Going it alone can be like trying to perform your own surgery. A financial planner is constantly required to update their skills in line with new rules and regulations. They can add value by identifying opportunities for investment, establishing the correct tax structure to suit your situation and tailoring a plan just for you.

ACTION

As life is constantly changing, it is very important to review your situation, investments and strategy on a regular basis – I suggest at least annually, depending upon your situation.

Below is a photo of our postcard board at Goals & Dreams Financial Planning Pty Ltd. We love to receive postcards from our clients. Our industry is full of compliance and lots of paperwork, but it is all worth it when we receive postcards from all over the world. It is such a great feeling to know that someone was thinking of us when they were in Portugal, Paris, Perth or Peru!

Figure 4. Postcard board at Goals & Dreams Financial Planning Pty Ltd

I have spent a great deal of time educating and enlightening my clients to take away the fear and uncertainty of investing. This is done in bite-size chunks in everyday language. I also challenge them to become more aware of the words they use and the thoughts they think and always encourage fun and laughter in our meetings and client gatherings.

2. Happiness

What is that elusive thing called happiness? I have done extensive reading on this subject since I was a teenager. I love the writings of Robert Holden and have been fortunate enough to meet him on a couple of occasions. Robert is a British psychologist, author and broadcaster who works in the field of positive psychology and wellbeing. He has written and recorded many books and audios which I strongly recommend you read and listen to.

In my experience, when I have been truly honest with myself, addressed the issues in my life that needed to be changed and *decided* to be happy no matter what was happening, that is when it happened. I was happy just by choosing to be happy and feeling grateful for what I had. As you have seen, I am a great believer in having positive messages around us to remind us to be happy and grateful.

I know without a shadow of a doubt that the more you focus on the negative and the things you *don't* want, the more of them you will receive. (Remember the elephant in the pink tutu?)

If you make a conscious decision today, right now, to no longer play the victim, things will change. Be the change you want to see, make a difference in your own life first, and then you will be much better equipped to help others.

3. Health

One of the saddest things to see is someone who has worked hard all their life, hoping to do all the things on their wish list in retirement, only to have illness squash all their dreams. You may have your finances sorted, but if you can't enjoy the fruits of all your hard work due to illness, it is of little comfort.

This is why your health is as important as your wealth. What did you eat for breakfast today? What exercise have you done in the past week? How much water do you drink each day? Think of a tiny newborn baby, all precious and brand new, fresh and sparkling, with a whole lifetime ahead of them. We were all like that once. Does a baby worry about having fat legs or a big bottom? We are all born with this amazing body that is so intricate and incredible in its design. However, do we care for it, nurture it and listen to it when it tries to tell us something?

Our miraculous bodies are able to repair and heal when we provide them with what they need. When making food choices, remember to read labels, buy fresh fruit and vegetables (preferably organic) and take a moment to find joy in the beautiful colours that nature provides. Move your body, whether it is walking, swimming, riding a bike or playing with kids. Do something that you enjoy. I love going to Zumba as I love music and love to dance. Get outside and enjoy the fresh air, breathe deeply and feel grateful for today.

4. Love

How much do you love yourself?

Do you spend enough time with the ones you love?

Do you tell your loved ones that you love them and are grateful for the things they do?

A great book on love is *The 5 Love Languages* by Gary Chapman. It explains that we all have different ways of showing others that we love them. When we appreciate that our loved ones may have a different love language to us, it helps both parties understand each other and communicate on a different level.

Love, life and relationships can be challenging. You may feel that it is hard to open your heart to others if you have been hurt in the past. Here is another opportunity to ask yourself if you are operating from a position of love or fear. If it is fear, what are you afraid of and why? Do you need to delve deeper into your own feelings, emotions and beliefs?

Think of how loyal our animals are – they love us just the way we are. My dog has always greeted me with such exuberance, even if I've only been gone for a couple of hours. He senses when I am sad as he feels my energy. Growing up on a farm, I had beautiful horses that would show their love every day with nuzzles of appreciation. The cows with their beautiful big brown eyes would give big licks of love as you gave them a pat. Love flows from many different sources.

Many of us long for the magic that is felt when we first meet someone and fall in love. The energy and vibes are incredible. I love to see some of my clients who have been married for over 50 years. They share knowing looks of love and still walk together holding hands. How blessed are they?

If you are in a loving relationship, are you doing enough to make sure the romance continues? Or do you let the mundane drudge of daily chores and life's challenges bring you down and you forget to feel grateful for what you have? We all need to nurture these special bonds.

Remember to love yourself first and the rest will follow.

5. Spirituality

Spirituality is a very personal thing. It has led me on an amazing journey of self-discovery and I know that there is an essence or higher self that is guiding me on my journey. Each person has their own beliefs and follows their own path. With so much greed and violence in the world, I have a deep-seated belief that somehow humankind may have lost the way. Yet, there is an abundance of kindness and goodwill, and acts of love and generosity around us every day, if we choose to see them.

Whatever your path is, may you follow it with love. My wish for you is that it is a path of love, happiness and fulfilment.

6. Family

The joy of having family around is such a blessing. Or, for some, a curse, depending upon the relationships in your family. I understand the dynamics of family life do not always run smoothly and the various personalities can be a challenge to deal with. People who are hurting often inflict pain on others, as they don't know any other way to express their feelings and emotions. Hurt people hurt people.

> **❝ Family does not necessarily mean the people we are related to. ❞**

I have a rather large extended family and for me it is such a joy to gather everyone together, sharing laughter and fun times. We have all been there for each other through tough times as well as fun times.

The fabric of life is based on our family values. Family does not necessarily mean the people we are related to. Often there are those we feel so close to that we invite them in to join our circle as they feel like family too.

Sometimes we get so caught up in the 'have to haves' that we forget the simple pleasures of being with the ones we love. We did not have a lot of money when I grew up and times were tough on the farm. Yet I recall the wonder I felt as a little girl when my dad would somehow make coins magically disappear in his arm. He would then pull the same coin from behind my ear. Or the times he would say, "Katie, come and sit on my knee."

When I was about three years old, Dad was pulling the mower apart and had the pieces all lined up in order. I thought it looked messy so I tidied it up. Dad looked at what I had done and, with his hand on his hip, he laughed. "Well, you're a bloody big help, aren't you?" he said.

I remember marching up the stairs so proudly to tell Mum what a good job I'd done. He could have been angry, yet he chose to just laugh.

My mum was such a blessing with all her help when my daughter Shelley was born. Shelley had reflux (think scenes from the movie *The Exorcist*) and had to wear a horrible brace (due to hip dysplasia). Shelley hardly slept more than 20 minutes, day or night, for the first nine months of her life, and I was like a walking zombie. My mum was there helping and offering support. Sadly, my mother passed away on my daughter's birthday in March 2017. I remember all the love she has given all my life.

Enjoy your family and loved ones. Have fun times, laugh lots and hug them.

7. Hobbies and fun

This is always an interesting question when I see my clients. I ask them the questions "What do you do in your spare time for fun?" and "Do you have any hobbies?"

It is so important to have an outlet or release that provides enjoyment and makes you feel alive. When my children were small, I used to make a lot of cross-stitch items for friends and family. I enjoyed it because it made me sit down and stop my busy life and there was a finished item at the end. I found one while cleaning up the other day and it would have been made about 27 years ago. As I picked it up, I remembered exactly what was happening in my life when I did the sewing. Aren't our minds incredible?

8. Career and success

People spend such a huge percentage of their life going to work to earn a living, and so many of them are desperately unhappy in the work they do. They get up every morning with fear and dread of what the day will bring. When someone is in this situation, they know they are unhappy but feel burdened with the weight and responsibility of having to earn this income to pay all the bills.

Over time, this unhappiness can impact our health and our relationships with family and friends. We can focus too much time away from what really matters in our lives. On the flip side, when we meet people who are following their passion, it oozes from the pores of their being. Their face lights up when they talk about what they do. They fill their days with upbeat energy and a bounce in their step.

Success should not be measured by the number of hours spent at your job or the wage you earn. If you are not happy, find something that fuels your soul. Take the step to get out of the rut, even if it is just a small step. Take it. Make a change. You are the author of the next chapter of your life.

> **“ Who you are in your working life is not the essence of who you really are. ”**

Who you are in your working life is not the essence of who you really are – it is a role you play that provides an income. I am blessed to love what I do, and I am passionate about making a difference in the world, little by little. Of course, we all need to have a sense of pride in the work that we do. Yet don't let it be the total focus of your life each and every day.

9. Friendship

Sit quietly and think of the wonderful people in your life who are your friends. I recall someone wrote in my autograph book at school: "True Friends are like diamonds, precious and rare. False friends are like autumn leaves, scattered everywhere."

How true is that? It obviously had an impact as I still remember the words. True friends are a blessing to our lives. They lift us up when we are feeling down. They are fun to be with and laugh at our jokes. They provide a hug and listen to our problems and wipe away the tears. They share a glass of champagne or a cup of tea and celebrate with us.

Perhaps you have friends in your life who just pour all their problems on you and walk away feeling better while you feel weighed down. If this is something that happens often, perhaps you need to consider if this is a mutually beneficial friendship with even amounts of giving and receiving.

You could also be a people pleaser and put everyone else's needs above your own.

If you have toxic people in your life, rethink the relationship and perhaps choose not to spend so much time with those who bring you down instead of lifting you up. To have beautiful friends, you need to be a kind, loving and generous friend as well. What goes around comes around. When you make the decision to remove friendships that are not beneficial, it is amazing how the cosmos responds and sends you beautiful new friends.

Creating your wish list

Something very powerful happens when we take the thoughts out of our head and write them down. They begin to take shape and form.

When I see clients who are couples in the office, I encourage them to write separate wish lists. I have been amazed how this has helped my clients' relationships, as they often find out things about the other that they didn't know. Communication is enhanced and they have fun finding out more about each other. In one of these discussions, one client found out that her husband wanted to go heli-skiing down the slopes in New Zealand.

The wish list is the starting point that directs the strategy to help you achieve your goals and dreams.

Goals and dreams

The following examples are provided to get you started. Remember, this is *your* life and this is all about you, and your goals and dreams may be different. Recreate these lists using your own examples and write them in your journal.

This is your life and you get to write the script.

Short term (12 months–2 years)

- Repay credit card
- Save for a holiday
- Enjoy weekends away
- Find a soul mate
- Have fun and enjoy life
- Learn belly dancing
- Wine and dine, and socialise with friends
- Be fit and healthy

Medium term (2–5 years)

- Buy a new car
- Take an overseas holiday to Paris
- Undertake further studies
- Visit Uluru
- Reduce home loan debt
- Start my own business
- Have fun and enjoy life
- Buy my first home

Long term (5–10 years)

- Be debt-free
- Travel overseas every two years
- Buy a home at the beach/mountains
- Buy beautiful jewellery
- Provide for children's education
- Provide for children's wedding
- Be fit and healthy

Longer term (10–20 years plus)

- Retire comfortably with peace of mind
- Travel the world
- Spend kids' inheritance
- Be fit and healthy
- Provide for grandkids' education

EXERCISE
Creating your wish list

Refer to the reality check chart and the goals and dreams list earlier in this chapter.

- Do you feel a little more optimistic about your life and the possibility that you *can* make things happen?
- Write your list!
- Include everything, no matter how big or small.

You can write the list however you like. You can start it with "One day I'd like to…" and write paragraphs, or you can just do dot points.

Many of my clients report back after doing this exercise that they didn't know they had so many things they wanted to do until they had given themselves the permission to dream.

Once this wish list is in place, you can begin to design what *action* is needed to help you achieve your goals and dreams.

Look at the things on your wish list. What can you start doing now?

Start doing more things that bring you joy – even if it is just going to the movies, walking on the beach, sailing or flying a kite!

ACTION

This delightful poem was sent by a client in appreciation of the advice they received, which is helping them achieve their goals and dreams. I was truly humbled when I read the words and realised what a difference the advice has made to their life!

Our 2023

Ending the year of 2022.
We handed our goals and dreams to you.
Whilst we were unsure at the start.
Your wonderful team played their part.
Our scattered funds were collected and sorted.
Growth and income duly reported.
We ended that year full of hope.
Jobless and retired, we knew we'd cope.
Our dreams were not big, amazing or grand.
Our wish list could be counted on just one hand.

We slept in late and read the news.
Deciding which breakfast? It was hard to choose!
No hurried Weetbix and out the door.
Now a leisurely breakfast and coffee x 4.
We indulged our hobbies and found a few more.
Although, our fisherman's luck is as bad as before.
It's nothing to do with the fisherman, you see.
And could be easily fixed with a 'Seadoo' jetski (apparently!).

HOW TO CREATE YOUR WISH LIST

We've camped on the beach and watched whales swim by.
Boarded planes and taken to the sky.
I've sat on the deck and read a good book.
Searched the internet for a recipe to cook.
We've ridden horses and hiked in the hills.
Fallen from a mountain bike, whilst enjoying the thrills.
There's time to relax and 'Just Be'.
No deadlines to meet, no clients to see.
Time still ticks by, just as before.
But now we're feeling that 'Less is More'.

The sun still rises and the stars still appear.
And we're loving it all – it's fun without fear.

> "The journey of a thousand miles begins with a single step."
>
> — Lao Tzu

10

Explaining Financial Planning

Wherever you are in the journey of life, it is never too late to make a change. Mentally draw a line in the sand and choose to move forward now! Don't waste another second procrastinating. You owe it to yourself to make a difference to your own life first!

ACTION

EXERCISE
Watch what you are saying!

Are you still saying any of the following?

- I'll never have any wealth.
- I'll never be able to travel.
- I'm hopeless at budgeting.
- I've never been good with handling money.

Remember, you can change your thinking by saying:

- *In the past*, I never had any wealth.
- *In the past*, I was never able to travel.
- *In the past*, I was hopeless at budgeting.
- *In the past*, I was never good with handling money.

Try it out! Break those bad habits!

As I have mentioned before, I am a woman in a male-dominated industry and my approach is not only based on numbers, but emotions and life experiences as well. We are all human beings and our thoughts and feelings do not discriminate whether we are male or female, although our brains are wired differently.

Choosing a financial planner

In Australia, there are strict standards and guidelines under which financial planners operate. If you decide to engage a financial planner, look for a financial planner who has Certified Financial Planner (CFP) accreditation. This is a certification provided by the Financial Advice Association Australia and ensures that the planner adheres to a code of ethics, standards and values, which is recognised worldwide.

In addition to knowledge, you must also be able to feel comfortable with your planner. There needs to be rapport and trust, and they need to be able to communicate with you in a language you understand. Some people are visual and like to see diagrams and illustrations. Others like to hear information explained as their dominant learning type is auditory. Engineers (by way of example) like to have all the information documented in clear and concise detail.

After many years of people watching, and observing and studying the psychology of money, I usually pick up the signs from the clients quickly and intuitively. Therefore, I make sure that when I have a couple sitting in front of me who are different learning and communication types, I explain the same thing in two different learning styles to ensure they both receive the information in the format they relate to.

This is the process we use at Goals & Dreams Financial Planning Pty Ltd.

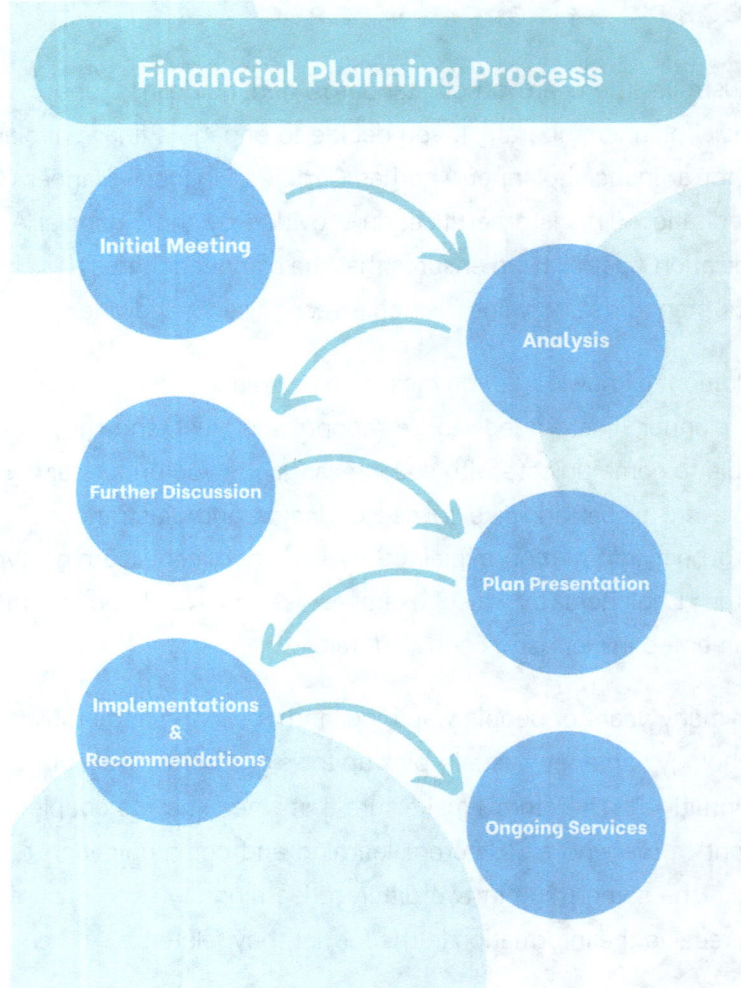

Figure 5. Financial planning process

Sometimes, if you don't know where to start or, for example, have a bit of a mess with various superannuation funds, the best place to start is to seek advice. I have no idea how to fix the engine in my car, so I seek the support and expertise of someone I trust.

EXPLAINING FINANCIAL PLANNING

A qualified financial planner can provide clarity and direction and assist you on your path. Recently, I was able to tell a long-term client that he can retire now – two years earlier than planned. He had a very stressful, high-pressure role and had had enough. He had tears in his eyes as he thanked me for giving him permission and for getting him into a position of financial freedom.

> **Money doesn't buy happiness; it just gives you more choices!**

Money doesn't buy happiness; it just gives you more choices!

Financial planning is like a jigsaw puzzle. Depending upon where you are on life's journey, what you need may be different from your neighbour, friends or family. What I am referring to here is that if you are in your 30s, married with three children and a mortgage, what you need is going to be very different from someone who is either just starting out or someone who is approaching or has reached retirement age.

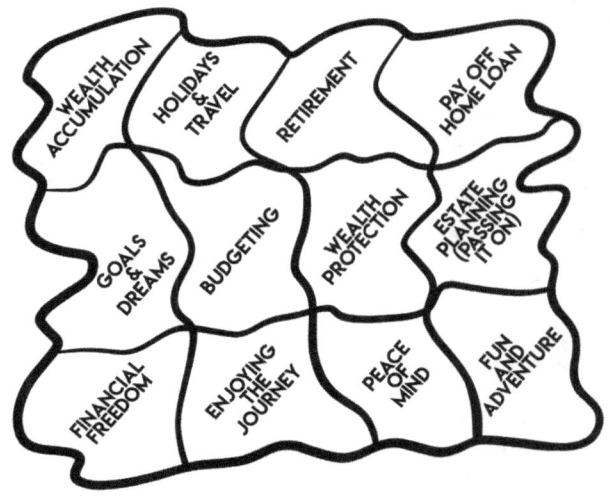

Figure 6. Financial jigsaw puzzle

"The visionary starts with
a clean sheet of paper, and
re-imagines the world."

— Malcolm Gladwell

11

Where Are You Now?

Now you know where you want to be. You have written your wish list and are ready to begin the next chapter of your life. You are excited with new direction and purpose.

What happens now?

It is crunch time. Before you move forward, you need to be totally honest and evaluate exactly where you are now. If you were sitting in front of me in my office, I would seek permission to ask you many questions. It always amazes me that when we go through the process, sometimes clients are absolutely gobsmacked when they realise that they are already millionaires. When we add up the value of their home, superannuation assets and investments, then take off any debt, the net figure represents their total wealth as a dollar figure. Most people aren't aware of this value.

Or alternatively, you know what your net worth is and you want to make a change.

This is where we do a stocktake of your current situation. What do you own? What do you owe?

- How much do you have in your superannuation/retirement fund?
- What income do you receive?
- What does it cost you to live? (I know, here comes that dreaded 'b' word for budget.)
- Do you have any surplus funds?
- Do you have enough to pay the bills?
- Are you covered if you have an accident or injury and can't work?
- Do you have death and disability insurance? If so, how much?
- Do you have health insurance?
- Do you have income protection?
- Who is nominated as your beneficiary for your superannuation fund? What type of nomination is it – binding or non-binding – and does it lapse?

- Do you have good debt or bad debt?
- Do you have any negative gearing and what actually is it?
- Do you have a will or enduring power of attorney in place?

Now let's explore the above in more detail.

EXERCISE
Assets and liabilities summary

Either copy the tables on the following pages into your journal or download them from www.goalsanddreams.com.au and list your assets and liabilities.

Imagine I am sitting in front of you, asking about your current position.

ACTION

ASSETS		Owner (Sole, Joint or Other Entity)	
Personal/Lifestyle		Owner	$
	Home		
	Contents		
	Cars		
	Other		
Bank accounts	Bank	Owner	$
Rental properties	Location	Owner	$
Australian shares	Shares (Company/ No of shares)	Owner	$
Managed funds	Investment	Owner	$

Superannuation	Who with	Owner	$
LIABILITIES			
Loans	Type	Owner	$
INCOME			
Salary	Employer	Owner	$
Centrelink	Type of pension/ Allowance	Owner	$
Other	Detail	Owner	$

Figure 7. Assets and liabilities summary

Where does your pay go?

A budget can seem daunting at first, however, it is very powerful. Once you know where your money is going, it helps you make informed choices about spending.

> **" Doing a budget helps to identify if you are living above your means. "**

Sitting just behind the wish list in terms of importance is the budget. Completing a budget is something that most people don't want to do. The budget is another component of crunch time as it is amazing how the dollars just seem to disappear from payday to payday if you aren't disciplined.

Doing a budget helps to identify if you are living above your means or if you should have surplus cash in your bank account.

This is the time for reality. Be honest with yourself. This is your life!

EXERCISE
Your budget

Either copy the table on the following pages into your journal or download it from www.goalsanddreams.com.au and list your expenses.

DETAILED REGULAR EXPENSES	WEEKLY	MONTHLY	ANNUAL	TOTAL PER YEAR
HOUSING				
Rent				
Home mortgage				
Council/shire rates				
Rates property 2				
Water rates				
Electricity				
Gas/Oil				
Telephone				
House & contents insurance				
Household repairs and maintenance				
Furnishing/Appliances				
HEALTH				
Health benefits/Insurance				
Chemist				
Medical/Dental/Optical				
TRANSPORT				
Running costs/Petrol/Fuel				
Registration/Third party				
Comprehensive insurance				

ACTION

DETAILED REGULAR EXPENSES	WEEKLY	MONTHLY	ANNUAL	TOTAL PER YEAR
Maintenance/Services/Repairs				
Licence fees/Fines/Parking				
Public transport/Taxi fares				
Loan/Lease repayments				
FOOD				
Groceries				
Meat				
Fruit & vegetables				
Lunches				
Alcohol & cigarettes				
EDUCATION				
School fees				
Child care				
Other				
PERSONAL				
Clothing/Footwear				
Entertainment/Dining out				
Sport/Recreation/Hobbies				
Haircuts				
Gifts/Presents/Christmas				
Vacations/Holidays				

DETAILED REGULAR EXPENSES	WEEKLY	MONTHLY	ANNUAL	TOTAL PER YEAR
Books/Magazines/Newspapers				
Subscriptions/Fees				
Life insurance				
Disability insurance				
OTHER				
Child support/Maintenance				
Pet/Vet fees				
Charities/Donations				
Miscellaneous				
TOTAL				

Figure 8. Budget

When I see clients face to face and we have discussed their situation, I write a homework list for them, which itemises the things they need to follow up on after our meeting. Depending on how much information they bring to the first meeting, the list varies in length. However, almost 95 per cent of the time nobody is aware of how much they need to live on each year. It is usually a shock when they tally it up. Some people are too scared to add it up.

As a financial planner, it is not my role to tell you that you can't afford Tim Tams (yummy Australian chocolate biscuits). But it is my role to encourage my clients to look at areas where they might be able to cut down. For example, I had a couple that earned very good incomes but money was slipping through their fingers. When they did their budget, they realised that they were spending $20 per day *each* on lunch and takeaway coffee. This equates to $200 per week (assuming a five-day working week). Discounting annual holidays of four weeks, they realised they were spending $9,600 per annum on these. They were both heavy smokers as well and were spending over $10,000 per annum in this area.

On their wish list, they both indicated that they wanted to lose weight and be fit and healthy. They decided to give up smoking and only buy lunch one day per week as a treat. This gave them ownership of their decisions and helped them make the choice themselves on how to make changes. With almost $20,000 per annum identified just in these areas, they became excited. Within just three months they proved that they were genuine in their desire to change the direction of their life. They had saved a huge amount and were able to cross off some of their short-term goals. We then identified what was a comfortable surplus to be able to work on their medium- to long-term goals.

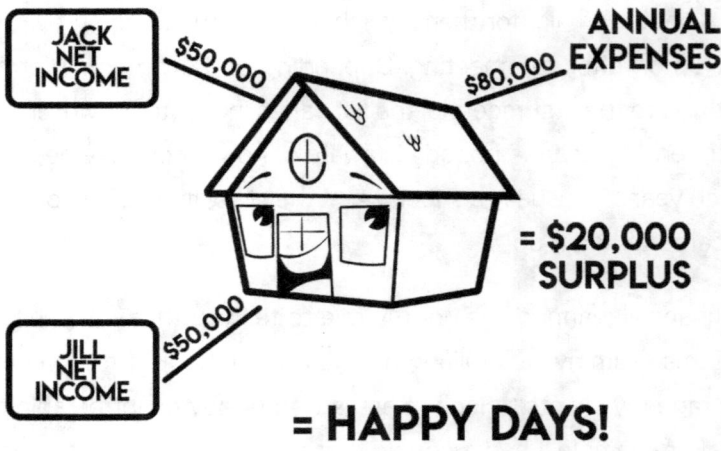

Figure 9.1 Jack and Jill

PETER & PAULA

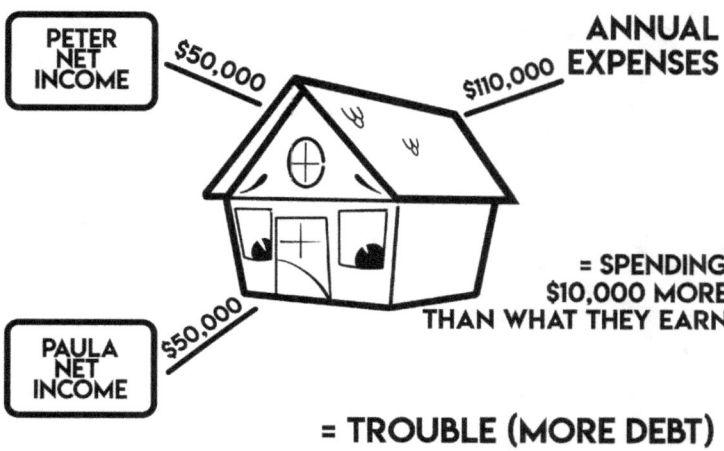

Figure 9.2. Peter and Paula

Is your situation a Jack and Jill or a Peter and Paula? What is your backup when life throws you an unexpected accident or illness?

This is where I suggest you list how much insurance cover you have. Many people have no idea how much they have or if they even have any. Most people have taken out insurance cover for their home, car or caravan. However, usually the important person or persons who earn the money to provide for life have little or no personal insurance cover. Here is the reality check which addresses this important piece of the puzzle (if you don't already have enough cover). Just consider what would happen to your loved ones if you were no longer here providing an income to help pay all the bills.

ACTION

EXERCISE

Insurance

What insurance do you have for yourself?

Make a list of all your personal insurances.

Do you have the following covers?

- Death
- Disability
- Critical illness/trauma cover
- Income Protection.*

For each policy, note:

- the amount of cover
- the premium
- the company you are insured with.

*For income protection insurance, also list the amount of cover, waiting period and the benefit period, ie. two years or to age 65

These insurance options are explained in further detail in the Personal Insurance section in Chapter 13.

Where is your superannuation and who have you nominated?

A nomination of beneficiary is the instruction for your superannuation fund to pass on your funds upon your passing.

EXERCISE
Superannuation

List all of your superannuation accounts and the beneficiaries you have listed.

List the percentage and type of nomination (binding or non-binding).

*Note: A nomination to a spouse or dependent child is tax-free in the hands of the beneficiary in Australia.

What type of debt do you have?

There are several types of debt. Do you have good debt or bad debt?

Good debt

Simplistically, good debt is one where you can claim the interest as a tax deduction against income received. For example, if you borrowed funds to invest in a rental property, the interest paid can be offset as a tax deduction against the income received.

Such loans are often structured as interest only to maximise the tax deduction.

Your financial adviser may also suggest you use negative gearing, which is an additional strategy in cases where the interest you are charged is more than the income you make on the investment. This is a useful tax minimisation strategy for some investors and is available in Australia at the time of writing.

Negative gearing example:

Rental property net income after expenses	= $15,000 pa
Investment loan $400,000 @ 5% interest only	= $20,000 pa interest
Difference	= $ 5,000 pa

The above example is provided as a guideline only and is not provided as taxation advice. Seek advice from a professional tax adviser should you wish to know more about this option.

Bad debt

A bad debt is any debt where you cannot claim the interest as a tax deduction. This usually happens with the interest on the loan for the home you live in, as it is not an investment loan and therefore cannot be claimed as a tax deduction. For this reason, it's important to pay down the debt on your own home quickly. You could do this by paying the principal and interest on the loan rather than the interest-only strategy that is used for investment property.

Credit card debt (really bad debt)

Credit cards can be a wonderful way to structure your finances if treated with respect and discipline. If you repay the amount owing in full every month, you are the winner. If you buy up using your card and then can't repay the full amount, the credit card provider is the winner. Despite interest rates being relatively low in Australia, some credit cards attract an interest rate of up to and in excess of 20%.

Likewise, many finance companies provide fast loans with rates in excess of 25%. Be careful.

Love letter from the grave (your will) and other important documents

Estate planning is an important part of financial planning and your life (a piece of the overall puzzle). You may have the best strategies or investments in place, however, if your estate planning issues are not in place it can all unravel.

EXERCISE

Your will

Do you have a current will?

- If so, who is the executor?
- Where is the will kept?
- Does a solicitor/lawyer have a copy? If so, what are the solicitor's details?

Do you have an enduring power of attorney?

- If so, who is nominated?
- Where is the document kept?
- Does it cover both financial and medical nominations?

If you don't have a will, how soon can you organise an appointment with your solicitor?!

By now, you may be feeling a little overwhelmed and it's time for a cuppa – or a beer or glass of wine!

Now you have done all the exercises in this chapter, what have you discovered?

- Do you earn enough to cover your living expenses, as identified in the budget and the diagrams re Peter and Paula and Jack and Jill?
- If you have surplus funds, do you make them work hard for you?
- If there is a shortfall, are there any areas where you can cut back?
- Are the things on your wish list achievable or do they seem impossible?
- Do you have a number of superannuation funds or just one, and do you have a nomination of beneficiary listed?
- Do you have enough personal insurance cover?
- Do you have a current will and enduring power of attorney?

If all these questions seem far too daunting or overwhelming, answering them will provide clarity and help you move forward. You may even be wondering what you do with this information now that you have it. One option is to seek the professional advice of a qualified financial planner, who will assist you in navigating the way forward. Any financial planner would welcome a client who arrives with all this detail already in hand.

Many of my clients have commented over the years that they knew these things were important, but they just never got around to doing them. When I write them a homework list, they suddenly become accountable and the list gets ticked off. I've even had a school principal say that it is a long time since anyone has given him homework.

I always tell my clients that they receive a gold star when they report back to me that they have done their homework. I have also been told many times by clients that they didn't know what they didn't know!

At Goals & Dreams Financial Planning Pty Ltd, we analyse all the information about your life, wish list and present situation – all the questions I have asked you here. There may be much deeper research required into your insurance, existing investments and superannuation funds, which we undertake on your behalf, as will any financial planner you see. The life of a financial planner is a moving feast of rules and regulatory changes and continuous upskilling of knowledge and experience. While I have the letters and qualifications after my name, my greatest learnings have come from working with real people for more than 35 years.

Your situation may be quite simple. You may have decided that you want to take a trip to Paris in two years' time. You have re-evaluated your budget and realised that if you cut back on some expenses and save $X, the goal is achievable.

I am all for enjoying the journey and encourage my clients to enjoy this beautiful world we live in. However, the key is to find the balance where you can enjoy your short- to medium-term goals while also investing for the long term, in order to provide financial freedom and passive income to enjoy many more adventures and experiences.

"Knowledge is power."

— Sir Francis Bacon

12

Knowledge – Face Your Fears

The next two chapters are where we start looking at the tools and vehicles that we might use to help you achieve your goals and dreams and tick off the things on your wish list. Imagine it as a funnel that filters down into the *how* we make your financial situation attune with your aspirations.

Think about when you have had a preconceived idea about something yet when you investigate it more deeply, your increased knowledge helps you make an informed decision more easily. When we go searching and delve into a situation, the search helps us determine what we definitely *don't* want. Armed with this insight, we can mentally turn our bodies around and visualise walking towards what we *do* want.

Alternatively, sometimes we become so stuck in the mindset of what we don't want that we have truly lost sight of what resonates with us and what we want to have, achieve, feel or be. The situation could be as simple as buying a new mobile phone. There are so many options, features and functions available these days, the choice can be overwhelming. However, once you focus on what features you require and work through the elimination process, it becomes easier.

The same principle applies to how you manage your money. You need the extra information to know what decisions to make.

When it comes to investing, there are those who are genuinely concerned about your wellbeing and there are those who do not have the best intentions when it comes to investing. In some of these instances, when someone in the finance world does the wrong thing, newspapers run headlines damning the whole industry.

Have you ever seen a headline "Happy clients send postcards to their financial planner"? Of course not. Only bad news sells newspapers and makes headlines. The financial planning industry has so many rules and legislative complexities and so much compliance it is overwhelming. This is meant to protect the consumer and I certainly understand why there is the need. The people who break these rules are the ones that headline in the papers, and it only takes one occurrence to send a ripple through an otherwise trustworthy community.

As a financial planner, when I become overwhelmed with the 'i' dotting and the 't' crossing, I simply go to the postcard board in our reception area. I stand there and refocus on why I do what I do, as the compliance and lengthy Statements of Advice (written recommendations such as a financial plan) are simply the vehicles to help my clients achieve the things on their wish lists.

Never let anyone steal your dreams.

In client meetings, many people come to me with opinions and ideas that have been passed onto them from family or friends, or even the guy at the pub! Sometimes a client's attitude towards money is one of lack, not abundance, and is fear based. When I take them through the learning process and increase their knowledge, they can make informed decisions and the fear is reduced. As they progress along the journey, piece by piece they are open to learning more and empowerment increases.

> **Never let anyone steal your dreams.**

How much do you know about investing?

The usual answer to this question is "Not much." Don't feel bad about this if that's your answer. I totally understand. Wherever you are now is a very good place to begin. Over time, many of my clients shake their heads and comment that they wish they had known all this 'stuff' when they were younger.

It is now a passion of mine to teach younger children, teenagers and young adults how to change their attitude towards money and wealth and take ownership. However, knowledge is not limited to the young and it is never too late to learn.

In a typical client-facing appointment, there is a lot of information to take in and at first it can seem overwhelming. I endeavour to present information in an easy to understand, bite-sized format. I have learnt that most people are visual and if I draw pictures, boxes and arrows, it helps their level of understanding increase. I'm not much of an artist, but the message appears to get through! Clients frequently ask to keep the piece of paper with my very basic drawings on it.

I have also learnt over time that, on average, approximately only 20% of our discussions will be retained from our first meeting. I always prefer couples to come in together, as it is very difficult for one person to go home and explain everything to the other. Also, different people hear different things and what a man takes in is often very different to what a woman does. However, as we progress on the journey, you can see the light bulb go off or the penny drop, and it all starts to become more familiar.

Are you getting the best out of your everyday bank accounts?

As I write these words, in Australia the official interest rate for cash has been very low for many years. However, rates are on the rise, which is fabulous if you are investing and challenging if you are borrowing. Similarly, across the world interest rates have been at all-time lows but are now on the rise. Switzerland's cash rate has been negative, which is mind boggling. However, times are changing and inflation is raising its ugly head, which means interest rates are increasing.

My advice is to simplify the number of bank accounts you have. To keep it easy to manage, have an everyday bank account into which your pay goes, and you use this account to pay for your everyday expenses. Use it to access EFTPOS and ATMs (in Australia). Depending upon how disciplined you are, you can keep reserves in that bank account to pay for bills as they come in. If you do this, make sure that you don't spend the money just because it is in the account. These types of accounts seldom pay you any interest.

If you need more discipline and want to separate funds for bills, open a separate higher interest account with your bank or institution. Most of the banks these days have online saving accounts that are linked to your everyday account. Interest is usually calculated on a daily basis and the cash is available whenever you want. However, ATM access is not usually available and you need to transfer funds from this account to your everyday account if you want to spend it.

Let's say you add up the total of your annual bills (refer to your budget!) and it comes to $5,200 per annum. If you are paid weekly, then you need to set aside $100 per pay into your bills account. If you are paid fortnightly, then the amount is $200 per pay. Imagine the feeling when the bill arrives and you have the funds to pay it straight away. Woohoo! It is an empowering feeling.

If you are saving for a personal goal, holiday, new car or something else, you may want to consider having a third (high interest) fun or goal account. Once again, if you need the discipline and you like to see the funds building up, you will enjoy the feeling when you are getting closer and closer. Having a 'don't touch' account requires focus, however, I have found that the bigger the goal and the more determined you are to achieve it, the discipline becomes easier. If you feel you are disciplined enough, just have the one separate, higher interest account.

Ensure you check with your own bank or institution for individual terms and conditions.

ACTION

What is an asset class and what are the risks involved with each one?

Let's take a deep breath here and delve in. This section is a bit intense. The terminology 'asset class' is used to describe the areas where we are able to invest, as follows:

- Cash and fixed interest/bonds – known as 'defensive assets'.
- Property, Australian shares and international shares – known as 'growth assets'.

You may be familiar with the pie chart usually shown on your superannuation or investment report. Figure 10 is a typical pie chart for a balanced investor (which represents 70% growth assets and 30% defensive assets).

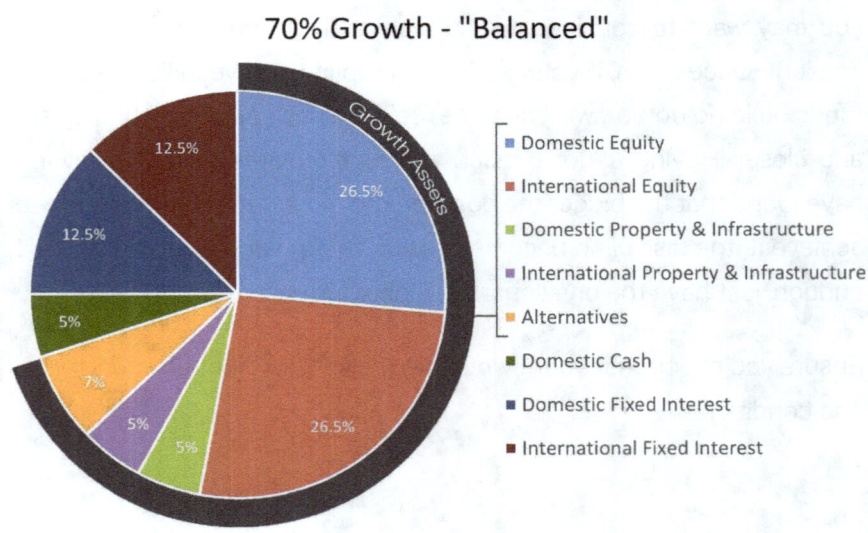

Figure 10. Balanced portfolio pie chart

Let's look at each asset class in turn.

Cash

This is the one we are most familiar with as our everyday banking is held in cash in a bank account. In the past, our grandparents or great grandparents may have stashed their hard-earned cash under the mattress as they didn't trust the banks. This often relates to the fear of what happened in the era of the Great Depression that started in 1929. This fear has often been passed down from generation to generation.

Many years ago, existing clients of mine arrived in my office with $30,000 cash which had been buried in the backyard and smelled musty and old. My poor assistant had never seen that much cash and had never counted that much money before. These days, the clients would have to take the funds to the bank and obtain a bank cheque or funds transfer via their bank account. How the world has changed.

Although interest rates paid by the banks and institutions are still relatively low, at least your money in a higher interest cash account can be earning something!

Risk

One of the major risks is that your money may not be keeping pace with inflation. In Australia, the average inflation rate over the last 30 years has been 3.19%. Therefore, you can see that if your funds are only earning, say, 1–2% at best, you are already behind the eight ball.

To keep pace with inflation, we need to have part of our funds invested in assets that will provide long-term capital growth.

Fixed interest, bonds and annuities

You may be more familiar with the description 'term deposit' to describe money invested in fixed interest. In my early banking days, it was also referred to as an 'interest-bearing deposit'. It relates to an investment that is held for a particular period of time and you are paid a fixed rate of return for that period.

For example, if you invested $20,000 x 12 months @ 2% interest, with the interest paid at maturity, at the end of the term, you would have your original capital plus interest of $400, which results in a total of $20,400.

Risk

While this is nice and safe and secure (depending on the stability of the institution where you invest), the downside is that you cannot access your capital during the time frame. Some banks do allow you to break the term deposit, however, there is usually a penalty involved. Also, the inflation risk also applies here.

As interest rate rises are happening now, there is a risk that you might invest your funds for a period of time and lock into the applicable interest rate, say, 4% x 12 months. If interest rates rise twice over that period of time you have missed out on the increase. On the flip side, if interest rates go down, you are the winner as you have the benefit of locking in the higher rate.

In periods where both interest rates and inflation are high, this also impacts the net result. Figure 11 is a graph showing the average income earned from a term deposit between 1980 and 2022 compared with the dividends from the share market. In each case, dividends have not been reinvested to compare apples with apples. As you can see, the term deposit capital value is still $100,000 and inflation has eroded the purchasing power. While the share market capital value has seen volatile times, the dividends continued to grow. This is due to the underlying companies' profits continuing to grow despite the volatility in the short term.

Of course, you always need to consider the strength of the business offering the term deposit. Often an organisation with a lower level of stability and credit rating will offer an investment with a higher rate to attract customers. Make sure you do your homework.

Shares vs term deposits

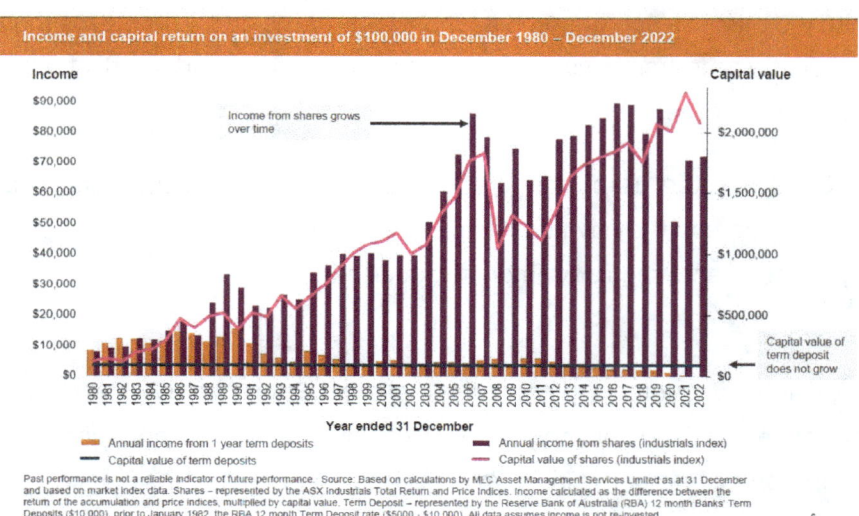

Figure 11. Shares vs term deposits.
I thank MLC Investments for permission to use this graph.

Annuities

An annuity is very much like a term deposit, however, you have the choice of several options.

You may select a five-year RCV100 annuity, investing, say, $100,000 @ 3%, with interest paid every six months. This means that each six months you will receive a payment of $1,500 until the end of the term and your original capital will still equal $100,000.

Another type is the RCV. The RCV stands for residual capital value.

RCV 100 means you have 100% of your capital (money) at the end of the term.

RCV 0 means – you guessed it – no capital at the end. This means that over the time frame, you may be paid both interest and part of your capital over the duration of the annuity.

RCV 0 is often used when you need to live using your capital and wish to spread the payments over a period of time so that you receive your payments regularly (monthly, quarterly, six monthly or yearly, for example)

An annuity quote is provided for clients before embarking on an investment (and of course, written advice which analyses the appropriateness of the investment for the client and their situation).

Risk

Annuities can be a wonderful strategy to sit alongside a portfolio of growth assets to ensure you are keeping pace with inflation. When interest rates are, say, 8%, the annuities can be a beneficial choice.

However, in times of lower rates and uncertainty about the direction of rates in the future, it may not be wise to lock into very long-term time frames.

There are types of annuities that also include a built-in increase, aligned with a CPI (consumer price index/inflation rate). It is always best to seek professional advice regarding such investments.

Lifetime annuities

As the name suggests, these annuities are taken over a lifetime and guarantee to pay an agreed amount over a lifetime. There can be various guarantee periods and you can nominate a beneficiary to receive any residual capital upon your death.

These types of annuities can be quite complex and there are many terms and conditions that apply. You should seek financial advice before entering such an investment to ensure it is appropriate for you.

Risk

Funds are locked away and you may be unable to access them in times of need. If funds *are* released, you may receive a lesser amount than was anticipated.

There is also an inflation risk as well. You may lock funds in at times of low interest rates, only to see the market change and rates rise, which usually means that inflation has risen as well.

As mentioned, these investments can be quite complex and require sound advice.

Bonds

Bonds are a form of debt. You loan a company or a government your funds and are promised all (or part) of capital will be returned at maturity and you will receive income along the way. It may seem safe and secure, however, like any investment, there are risks associated. It is wise to seek sound investment companies with a long-term track record.

Risk

As you are usually rewarded for taking a higher risk with any investment, you need to feel comfortable that the company will be able to pay back your capital at the time of maturity. Bonds can be just as volatile as the share market, and it would be wise to seek an investment manager with an impressive track record and spread your funds across a portfolio of various bonds with high credit ratings.

Australian shares

There is often a lot of fear attached to investing in the share market. Yes, it can be scary and the media is renowned for sensationalising the gloom and doom aspects.

> ❝ There is often a lot of fear attached to investing in the share market. ❞

Everything we do daily involves the share market. Where you buy your groceries is more than likely a big company listed on the share market (like Coles or Woolworths). Branded items like your toothpaste, razors, fridge and washing machine are also likely on the share market. The list goes on. These companies run with the focus on making a profit and growing their business.

As a shareholder, you become a part-owner of a piece of that company and get to share in both the growth and the income (known as dividends). These types of investments need to be used as a long-term investment (unless you are a daily share trader).

While the value of a particular share may fluctuate many times on a daily basis, it does not reflect the true value of the company's operating profit. The short-term fluctuations are often driven by emotion and market sentiment.

Let's look a little further into share prices and the dividend or yield provided.

Here is an example:

- In January 2017, the Commonwealth Bank of Australia (CBA) share price was $85.00 and was paying income/dividends of 4.95% (higher than bank interest at the time, hey?).
- In the previous 12 months, the lowest price of the shares was $69.22 on 14/9/2016. The highest was $85.65 in January 2017.
- These prices can fluctuate in the short term. However, the income is still being paid. That is because the CBA is still a large company (known as a blue chip share), paying a dividend and making a profit.
- On 5/1/2007, the CBA share price was $48.47. On 30/9/1991, the share price was $6.74.
- At time of writing (January 2024) the share price is $114.24.

Therefore, if you forget about the short-term volatility and invest for the long term, you can benefit from a higher level of income and growth (as the share price continues to increase over time).

I'm sure you have all watched the news on television at night and heard that the Australian share market moved up, down, sideways, etcetera today. The All Ordinaries (known as the 'All Ords') commenced in 1980 and is a measure of the movement of the top 500 companies in the Australian share market.

We also have the benefit in Australia of companies paying franked dividends (also known as imputation credits). This means that the company pays tax (currently 30%) on the profit it makes before the dividend is paid to you. This means that if you are currently paying tax at a marginal tax rate of 37% (without Medicare levy, to keep it simple), you only have to pay the remaining 7%. If your tax rate is lower than 30%, you will receive a refund. Woohoo!

While the Australian share market provides many opportunities, our market represents less than 2% of the global market.

International shares

The same principles apply with international shares, however, the dividends are usually not as high as those paid in Australia.

Many large companies (for example, Nestlé or Apple) that have traditionally operated from either America or Europe are now based in many Asian countries as they see opportunity there.

Many years ago, Harvey Norman in Australia was considered a smaller company. On a recent trip to Singapore, I saw there was a large Harvey Norman store operating. The company has grown and no longer belongs to the smaller company stable.

As the Western world is impacting Asia, this flows through to various companies. For example, BMW sales have increased in China as more affluent Chinese are choosing to drive more luxury cars.

There are so many layers and levels that we can delve into in this area. However, I am endeavouring to keep it interesting and not too boring. With my clients we gradually build on the knowledge over time – when they are ready to receive more information. Otherwise, it can be totally overwhelming.

Risk

Of course, there are risks involved. Not all companies have solid asset backing, strong cash flow and balance sheets, pay high dividends and continue to grow. In the mining sector, investing in speculative companies has seen many people profit while others lose due to the risk associated with finding oil or precious metals.

If you are looking for a quick profit, I suggest that investing in the share market is not for you (unless you fancy yourself as a trader, as mentioned before).

However, in these times of low interest rates, many clients are drawn to the high dividend levels paid by blue chip Australian companies.

When investing overseas, another area of risk is currency movement, which can provide both gains and losses. There is also the country's political risk and stability of government to consider. Then there is Mother Nature and how unexpected earthquakes, tornadoes, cyclones, volcanoes and flooding can impact companies' profits.

The Diversification section in Chapter 13 offers further insight regarding options available to reduce risk.

Property

In Australia, it is very much part of our culture to own your own home. It is something you can see, touch and feel and there is a sense of solid foundation.

However, for the younger generations, it is becoming increasingly harder to save the deposit to purchase a home of their own. Families usually require two incomes to be able to service a home loan.

Often when people have repaid a reasonable portion of their home loan, they use this equity to be able to purchase a rental property. Many are lulled into a false sense of security when they say they own three rental properties. Congratulations if you do, but usually there is a substantial debt that is attached to the investments.

Things you must consider when purchasing a rental property (also known as 'direct property') are the costs associated, stamp duty, legal costs and other fees and charges. You must also consider the rent received less management fees (unless you manage this yourself), rates, insurance, body corporate fees and so on. Often when I work out these numbers for clients the rental income return can be less than 2%. This means you are taking a big risk for a smaller return and usually having to borrow funds as well.

I have many clients with fantastic rental properties and excellent tenants, and they are receiving both solid income and long-term capital growth.

Other types of direct property include industrial sheds, warehouses and business premises. The outlays for these types of properties are usually much higher than residential property.

Risk

If you have capital tied up in a rental property and need to access cash, you can't sell the bathroom or the bedroom.

The downside of purchasing direct property is the risk of having bad tenants who trash the property or don't pay their rent – the tenants from hell! I've also had clients who owned a rental property in a unit complex. There was a problem with the plumbing in the unit above and water leaked into my client's unit. There was a huge dispute with the body corporate about whose responsibility it was to fix. The impact was a lot of stress for my client as the existing tenants had to move out until the dispute was settled and the repairs made. This was extremely stressful for the owners as they did not have any rent coming in.

I recall an elderly gentleman who came to me many years ago. He already had an industrial shed which had been providing sound income. He said to me that he was a very conservative investor, however, he had borrowed a large sum of money to purchase the shed. When the tenants moved out, he could not find new tenants and had to continue making the loan repayments without the benefit of rental income. This depleted the capital reserves he had set aside for retirement. From my point of view, I considered borrowing such a large amount a risky strategy at his stage of life, as it meant putting many of his eggs in the one basket.

However, like any investment there are the good stories as well as the bad. The secret is to carefully choose the area where you purchase and do your homework when purchasing a property.

> "An investment in knowledge
> pays the best interest."
>
> — Benjamin Franklin

13

More Investment Options

In this chapter, we provide further information to guide you through the journey to help you make informed decisions.

What is a managed fund?

A managed fund is where a team of analysts and fund managers do research into various investments, decide if it is beneficial to invest and make the decisions about when to buy and sell. They are always looking at prevailing conditions, opportunities and market factors that may impact the investment. However, they do not have crystal balls and are still subject to unexpected events having an impact on the fund.

They usually have investment parameters that govern their decisions. For example, if it is an Australian share fund, they may invest, say, up to 90% of the assets of the fund in Australian shares with up to 10% in cash to provide liquidity (access to funds).

An international share fund may have investments all over the world or relate to a specific sector or country, such as Asia.

The fund managers/analysts visit the companies they invest in, speak to management, ask lots of questions and look at cash flow, profitability, future projects and other details. Most of us (as individual investors) do not have the time nor expertise to be able to do such extensive research.

Such funds might invest in 50–100 different companies under the one fund umbrella. Yes, the managed funds do charge fees, however, the long-term benefits of diversification and expertise provided are proven to provide sound long-term returns.

The value of the underlying assets within the fund are represented in a unit price, which may fluctuate on a daily basis.

For example. You may have 1,000 units in a fund with a unit price of $1.11, so your value on that day = $1,110.00.

Diversification

In the previous chapter, Figure 10 depicts a diversified portfolio that invests across all asset classes. The example provided shows what is known as a balanced portfolio which holds 70% in growth assets, such as Australian and international shares and property. The remaining 30% is invested in what is known as defensive assets, such as cash, fixed interest and bonds.

Now, let's break it down even further. For each asset class, it is best to spread your hard-earned dollars across various investments.

Using Australian shares as an example, let's say you wanted to invest $100,000 into the Australian market. Let's look at the following options:

1. You invest the total $100,000 in one company (say Telstra or one of the major banks). Therefore, all your capital is invested in the one company.

2. You invest the $100,000 in a managed share fund. This provides enhanced diversification, as that fund may invest in up to 50–100 different companies.

3. You spread your money across three managed funds. These funds each have different goals. One may be looking for the best income and franked dividends, the second may target the best long-term growth and the third might be looking at smaller companies that they believe may be mispriced and have sound long-term potential.

Now, let's say each of those options provided a net return of 10% (including income and growth). On the face of it, it seems that it doesn't really matter as you achieved the same result.

However, with the first option you took a much bigger risk by placing all your eggs in one basket. If that company got into trouble your investment is going to go down the gurgler as well.

The second option reduces your risk as you are now investing in more companies.

However, the third option provides the most diversification as now your money is spread across many more companies in various sectors. So, you took the *least* amount of risk to obtain your return.

There is a technical term called 'negative correlation' which explains what is achieved when you invest in different styles of investment, even within the one asset class. We could delve much deeper into this as there are many more layers of technicality and analysis, however, this is not meant to be a study book.

If you take this concept further and apply it to all the various asset classes, you achieve more diversification as you have invested in many different investments and options, thereby reducing the risk you are taking.

Dollar cost averaging

Dollar cost averaging is a fantastic way to increase your investments on a regular basis. It provides discipline and smooths the risk of investing in a volatile market.

> ❝ Dollar cost averaging is a fantastic way to increase your investments on a regular basis. ❞

This type of facility may be established to regularly contribute an amount that has been chosen on, say, a monthly basis. You nominate your bank account and establish an authority, and the funds are regularly withdrawn each month and added to the investment. For busy people, this is a fantastic way to be able to increase your wealth little by little over the long term.

Earlier in this chapter, I provided an example of owning 1,000 units in a fund with a unit price of $1.11. Using that amount as a base, let's see how dollar cost averaging may operate in practice.

MONTH	INVESTMENT	UNIT PRICE	UNITS PURCHASED	TOTAL UNITS	DOLLAR VALUE
JANUARY	$1,110.00	$1.11	1,000.00	1,000.00	$1,110.00
FEBRUARY	$100.00	$1.08	92.59	1,092.59	$1,180.00
MARCH	$100.00	$1.07	93.46	1,186.05	$1,269.07
APRIL	$100.00	$1.10	90.91	1,276.96	$1,404.66
MAY	$100.00	$1.12	89.29	1,366.25	$1,530.20
JUNE	$100.00	$1.09	91.74	1,457.99	$1,589.21
JULY	$100.00	$1.13	88.50	1,546.49	$1,747.53
AUGUST	$100.00	$1.07	93.46	1,639.95	$1,754.75
SEPTEMBER	$100.00	$1.08	92.59	1,732.54	$1,871.14
OCTOBER	$100.00	$1.11	90.09	1,822.63	$2,023.12
NOVEMBER	$100.00	$1.14	87.72	1910.35	$2,177.80
DECEMBER	$100.00	$1.17	85.47	1995.82	$2,335.11

Now, let's look at the situation in five years' time based on the above figures without any further investment or purchase of units. The unit price has now grown to $1.72. Therefore, if we have 1,995.82 units x $1.72 = current value is now $3,432.81. This represents an average return of 8% over the 5 years. During this time, the unit price would have fluctuated up and down on the journey, however, it is significantly higher than the original price of $1.11.

The two enemies when investing

The two things to be very aware of when investing are taxation and inflation.

> **The two things to be very aware of when investing are taxation and inflation.**

Taxation is more prominent in our minds as we pay our taxes every year. Many clients have said to me over the years that they don't trust superannuation due to bad press and rule changes. While it is true that the Australian Government have made many changes to superannuation in my 30-plus years as a financial planner, it is still a very tax-effective way to accumulate wealth.

The performance of a superannuation fund is determined by the underlying investment and management of the fund.

If we had identical portfolios invested:

1. Under the superannuation umbrella, the super fund earnings would be taxed at 15%.

2. A client on the highest marginal tax rate would be paying 45% (plus Medicare Levy).

Taxation is a very complex area and there are many alternative structures, trusts and arrangements under which your investments can be placed.

Each individual's situation should be assessed and a plan created and tailored for their specific needs.

Financial planners are not able to provide taxation advice and, likewise, accountants are not able to provide financial advice unless either party is qualified to do so. However, I have found that when an accountant, financial planner and solicitor or lawyer can all liaise with each other on behalf of the client, the best outcome is achieved.

We may be aware of inflation and can share stories of what our wages were when we first started working and what the cost of a car or house was then compared to now.

Inflation is that sneaky little fellow that just ticks away behind the scenes to increase prices. Therefore, we need our investments to ensure that they at least keep pace with inflation, and at best outperform inflation. This means that you need to have investments that not only provide income but also provide long-term capital growth as well.

If you refer to Figure 11, the graph comparing a term deposit to the share market, you will see the term deposit value is still $100,000 and of course the purchasing power has been eroded. While the share market has been volatile over the same time period, it has provided sound long-term capital growth. This, in turn, has therefore provided a hedge (protection) against inflation.

Did you know that the same trolley of groceries that cost $200 in 1990 cost approximately $479 in 2023?

Figure 12. Grocery trolley

Making sound investment decisions

Often life hands us unexpected challenges, and suddenly:

- our role has been made redundant
- our relationship breaks down
- a death occurs in the family
- accident or illness strikes
- the mining boom that we thought would go on forever has lulled.

Over all my years as a financial planner, there have been many occasions when I have seen clients at a very emotional and stressful time in their lives. We all know how it feels when your head and your heart are having a battle and it is difficult to think clearly. I always have a box of tissues on hand.

My advice is always the same. I show them that we are going to physically pick up the emotion and place it aside in a bubble of its own for the time being. We then look at the numbers associated and let the numbers do the talking (with guidance of course).

While I certainly have empathy for what they are going through, my clients tell me how comforting it was to have someone who could think rationally and sensibly without the cloud of emotion. Having said that, there have been a number of times that the challenges were so big for them that I was teary-eyed as well.

The primary fear is usually that they will make a wrong decision and put their financial future at risk.

When making financial decisions, be aware of letting emotion rule your decisions.

Who makes the investment decisions?

In most partnerships, there is usually one person who is more involved with the financial decisions than the other.

When I see new clients who are a couple, it is very important that they both be present and listen to what is being said.

The divorce courts are filled with people who haven't communicated well in their relationship and often money is one of the underlying factors.

> **When I see new clients who are a couple, it is very important that they both be present and listen to what is being said.**

ACTION

The challenge faced when it is left to one person is escalated when that person either dies or leaves the relationship. Not only do they have sadness and grief over the loss, but the partner is suddenly left floundering with having to now make financial decisions and some are unable to cope.

Both parties need to become more aware of what is happening with their joint financial situation and discuss the issues *together*. If one person is in charge of paying all the bills, discuss them with your partner. I suggest having a spreadsheet on your computer or using an exercise book where you record where the various bank accounts are and how the bills are being paid, whether it's over the counter, online or via direct debit.

I usually supply my clients with various investment articles as part of my clients' homework lists. This comes after I have explained the basics. It helps them feel more involved in their decisions. By increasing levels of knowledge in this area you will feel more empowered to see opportunities where others are fearful.

I often explain to clients that I will take care of the structure and direction of their financial situation and ensure that they have the appropriate advice to achieve their goals and dreams. However, if their portfolio goes up, mine goes up; if theirs goes down, so does mine. We are all in this together.

Estate planning

What does 'estate planning' mean? Estate planning is used to describe wills and enduring power of attorney (EPOA).

Will

Now, most of us know what a will is, however, how many have a current and valid will in place that reflects your wishes? You work hard to create your wealth, and it can all become unravelled if you haven't addressed this important issue. Of course, none of us wish to face the reality that someday we will no longer be here. Some will enjoy a long life with many blessings along the journey. Others may be taken too early with many of their dreams left behind. The truth is that one day you won't be here, and I'm sure you want your family to have a smooth transition when dealing with your estate. Remember, they will have grief to deal with which will be hard enough on its own. They won't need a legal drama or mess to sort out as well.

With the divorce rate so very high these days, establishing a new will is often forgotten in the process. Then you may meet someone new and remarry, and your family may become the 'Brady Bunch'. I have seen so many loving families become unravelled due to differing opinions about who should receive what and how much. A friend of mine who is a specialist in estate planning organises family meetings with the person making the will to address all issues openly and honestly while the person is still alive so they can give their opinion. While this is very brave, I agree totally that it is much better to address issues now, even though we often would prefer to put them in the too-hard basket.

One of my young clients who is 25 has secured a well-paid position after studying to become an engineer. He came to see me to ensure that he didn't let his newly secured high income slip through his fingers. He was rather astounded when I suggested that he needs to have a will and EPOA. "But I'm too young," he said. However, after he thought about it, he realised the truth in my advice. He laughed and said that I was making him put his grown-up pants on!

Superannuation nominations

Another thing to consider is who you have nominated as a beneficiary for your superannuation (if you live in Australia). Many people give their superannuation statement a cursory look when it comes and throw it in the drawer. When I point out to people that they still have their ex-husband or ex-wife nominated as the beneficiary, the colour drains from their face.

Non-binding

This type of nomination is a direction to the trustees of the superannuation fund about how you would like the value (which may include insurance) of your fund to be disbursed. However, if someone feels they are entitled to receive all or a portion of the benefit, they can challenge the nomination. This may hold up proceedings of payment of the benefit for a long time and your original wishes may not be fulfilled.

Non-lapsing binding

A non-lapsing binding nomination is a very clear direction to the trustees of the superannuation fund to follow through with your nomination and this cannot be challenged. The nomination continues until you choose to change it. In blended family situations, I strongly suggest that you are very clear in making your decision about your nomination. I also suggest that you seek professional advice regarding the tax implications of various nominations. Currently (in Australia), a spouse and/or dependent children are entitled to receive the superannuation benefit tax-free.

Some superannuation funds also have binding nominations, which also have a time frame (ie. three years). At such a time, the nomination must be reviewed and the documentation reissued, completed, signed and witnessed.

However, if you wish to apply a new nomination, you can do so at any time.

Enduring power of attorney (EPOA)

As I am a financial planner and not a legal expert, the following information is only a guide. Seek professional legal advice to have your will and an EPOA arranged.

An EPOA is a separate document to the will and may be called upon while you are alive. As soon as you pass away, it becomes null and void.

Nominating someone as your EPOA must be considered carefully and it must be someone you trust. For example, if you had an accident and were in hospital, you don't want your attorney to raid your bank account, using the EPOA as authority. On a more pleasant discussion, you may be going overseas for a period of time and you need someone to be able to act on your behalf, either for a set period of time or until you decide to nominate someone new.

Couples usually nominate each other (each person requires their own EPOA). However, it would be sound practice to have another person or persons nominated in case both people were in an accident. You can nominate the person to be able to act on their own or jointly with another person.

I recall clients of mine at their review meeting many years ago. They said, "We are going to rouse Kath! We still haven't done our EPOAs. But we will get around to it." Shortly after, the wife was diagnosed with a serious illness and was in hospital very ill. Her husband was distraught and was endeavouring to do things on her behalf. Even though he was her husband, there were things he couldn't do. He came into my office very distressed with tears in his eyes. He said to me, "Please tell all your clients to get that #!#!#! bit of paper organised!" So I do! Fortunately, she has recovered and they continue to enjoy every day of this precious life we are given.

An advanced health directive is a specialised document that provides authority for a nominated person to make decisions regarding your medical situation and treatment should you be unable to do so.

If you leave this part of the puzzle out, it can see all your hard work, goals and dreams come tumbling down. I am sure we have all seen situations that have torn families apart at an already very sad time.

If your life situation changes, ensure you review and update these important documents.

Personal insurance

Having sufficient personal insurance cover is critical. We all insure our house and contents and our car. Yet, we are the most important asset we have and our ability to earn money may be taken away by an unforeseen illness or accident.

Just imagine if you have all these wonderful goals and dreams and it is all based on your ability to earn $xyz in the coming years. Let's say you are 30 now and plan to retire at age 60. If you currently earn $60,000 per annum (without any pay increases to keep it simple) your earning capacity over that time frame is $1,800,000. Woohoo – it sounds a lot, doesn't it? What happens if you have a serious accident and can't work again? Or perhaps you have an accident or illness and need 1–2 years away from work. Those bills will keep coming in. Will you have enough to pay all your bills?

> **Having sufficient personal insurance cover is critical.**

If you are married with children, both the husband and wife need to have enough cover to provide for their families in their absence. As most households now rely on two incomes, what position do you want your family to be in if you aren't there to provide for them? Would you like the mortgage repaid and funds coming in to pay the bills or at least cover the income you were earning? If one partner is the stay-at-home carer of the children and something happens to them, will there be enough money to hire someone to help, allowing the remaining parent to be able to continue to go to work?

While we certainly hope that none of these situations ever happen to us, statistics tell us otherwise. Nobody wants the stress of accident or illness, but imagine the extra stress when you add money worries as well. In my career I have seen many sad situations that have been eased as financial worries are taken care of via insurance. Fortunately, the partner thought enough of their loved ones to provide for them in their absence. It is like a love letter from the grave.

Unfortunately, most Australians are underinsured and believe that nothing will ever happen to them. Life happens and often hands us unexpected situations or experiences. If the financial stresses are relieved via insurance, it provides peace of mind and certainty for your loved ones.

There are several different types of insurance available in Australia.

Death cover

This is self-explanatory. Death cover pays a lump sum to your nominated beneficiary or estate in the untimely event of your death.

Disability cover

Should you have an accident or illness and are unable to return to work, this type of cover can provide a lump sum to cover living expenses, medical expenses, rehabilitation and perhaps a new home if required. There are many types of cover in this area, and it is always best to seek the type of cover that will provide a benefit if you are unable to continue working in the profession for which you are trained. By way of example, if you were a neurosurgeon and severely damaged your hands, you would no longer be able to perform surgery. In this case, the type of cover needed to cover you is 'own occupation'. Some types of cover only pay out if you are unable to continue working in 'any occupation'.

Income protection

This type of cover provides a benefit should you have an accident or illness and are unable to work. In Australia, the benefit usually covers up to 75% of your normal income. The waiting period you choose determines the premium. When considering this type of cover, think about how long you would be able to survive and pay the bills should your income cease. Waiting periods start from as little as seven days and range from 30 to 90 days. Often this type of cover is held in a superannuation fund where the benefit time is limited to two years. It may be possible to have this cover in place together with a second policy outside superannuation with a waiting period of two years and a possible benefit period of up to age 65.

Critical illness and trauma cover

This type of cover provides a benefit should you become seriously ill or have an accident. It pays a lump sum which can cover many unforeseen expenses. I have known many people who have health insurance cover find that there is a gap between the cover provided and what the doctors, medication and treatment cost. Even the cost of hospital parking can put a hole in your pocket. My friend who was terminally ill used this benefit payment to take her children to Disneyland before she died.

The above information is a very broad overview and is included just to get you thinking about this important piece of the puzzle. On many occasions after an unexpected life occurrence has happened, I have seen the wonderful relief on clients' faces when they know they will be financially secure because they have insurance cover. It doesn't take the sadness away, however, it does reduce the financial stress and restores a sense of calm as they are able to provide for their family and loved ones.

> "Books aren't made of pages and words. They are made of hopes, dreams and possibilities."
>
> — Unknown

14

Stories of Success

The following are various scenarios and real-life cases (with names changed) depicting clients from different age groups to show examples of what can be achieved when you take action and move away from fear-based decisions.

Teenage years – James

James is in his 20s. However, this story began when he was just 14. James has always had a healthy respect for money and has been a good saver from when he was very little. He showed signs of being an entrepreneur at the age of eight. Unbeknown to his mother, he was buying $2 watches from the local bargain store and selling them at school for $5. At age 13, he wanted to change his school bank account to a higher interest account and already had worked out how much the increased interest would be. James is a very quiet young man and a deep thinker.

When James was 14, Goals & Dreams held a client seminar called Markets, Memories and Merriment. At that stage I had clocked up 21 years as a financial planner, and as my clients are quite a social bunch, they kept asking when we were having a twenty-first birthday party. We decided to combine this with a market update from an economist (right at the beginning of the Global Financial Crisis), a trip down memory lane with photos, TV shows, music and a comparison of what things cost now and what they cost back in 1987. The merriment part is self-explanatory and was lots of fun. James accompanied his family to this seminar and quietly took it all in.

A few months after this function, James and I had a conversation where he said, "Investments are really cheap now, aren't they? Can you please set up a little portfolio for me with the $2,200 I have saved?" Wow, he had been listening and paying attention! At this stage, James was also mowing lawns and doing odd jobs and we organised for $100 per month to be added to the investment via direct debit so it just happened automatically. This means he was taking advantage of dollar cost averaging.

The investment started in May 2009 and in January 2020 he had accumulated a total of $27,264, which has provided an average rate of net return of 9.19% (since inception) in very volatile times. In total over that period of time he has contributed a total of $17,265 (which includes the original $2,200, the monthly $100 contributions and all dividends reinvested). Along the journey he has withdrawn a total of $3,500 to fund the purchase of a new computer and assist with car repairs.

James is now working full-time and contributing to his fund and has a very healthy balance. His long-term return (since inception) to time of writing has been 8.70% net of all fees.

This just demonstrates the power of discipline and having a long-term view. I often share this story with my clients who have since organised their children or grandchildren to start a similar investment portfolio. So many of my clients have commented that they wish they knew these options when they were younger.

I truly believe this knowledge and education should be provided in schools and have volunteered in the past to speak at high schools to teach our young adults the skills they need to thrive in the real world.

Twenties – Amy and Adam

Amy and Adam are a young couple who have recently married. They are good savers and want to get ahead in life and are currently saving for their first home. They want to protect themselves and each other should anything unforeseen happen, so wanted information regarding personal insurance. While focusing on their present goal, they also wanted to make sure their future is secure. They are interested in tax savings (via salary sacrifice and salary packaging). They have each established a will and an EPOA and understand the importance of these legal documents.

They are also interested in creating an investment portfolio for the long term, separate from their superannuation. They now feel confident and empowered that they are on track to achieve the things on their wish list. Amy and Adam commented, "We didn't know what we didn't know," before seeking professional financial advice.

Thirties – Fiona and Guy

Fiona and Guy are married with three children, have a mortgage and are trying to keep their heads above water. They have a very busy life. They were struggling to make ends meet and felt they just weren't getting anywhere.

They both work full-time and earn good incomes. We worked with them to analyse where the 'leaks' in their budget were. These leaks were negating any potential for savings. Once they took ownership of their decisions and we guided them through the numbers, Fiona and Guy now feel that they are working towards achieving their goals.

They had a couple of rather large credit card debts and felt that all their time and energy spent working and juggling a young family wasn't getting them anywhere. They had some equity in their home loan, so we organised to repay the quite substantial credit card debt using this equity. They retained one card with a reduced limit and now repay in full whatever has been spent every month. While they still have debt, the interest rate reduced from 20% to the current market rate (considerably lower). They are paying extra into their home loan to reduce the debt, however, they now have spare funds which are being channelled into savings for their goals and items on their wish list.

Their mortgage is now under control and they are on track to take the children to Disneyland, which previously just seemed like a pipedream. Fiona and Guy feel so much more empowered and in control of their own destiny. They promise to send a postcard!

Forties – Tracey and Geoff

Tracey and Geoff are in their mid-40s and are empty-nesters who are fully focused on enjoying life. This newfound freedom is exhilarating; however, they are also really looking at retirement in a different light as it draws closer.

With the absence of school and university fees, they suddenly have surplus cash flow and want to enjoy the journey while ensuring the fun will last into retirement.

Within a short period of time:

- their mortgage was repaid
- funds were going into superannuation for long-term savings
- we put another investment strategy in place to save tax and grow their wealth should they wish to retire before they can access their superannuation investments (due to government-set retirement ages).

Now they have an overseas trip every second year and are on track to retire early.

Fifties – Jan and Michael

When we met Jan and Michael, they were pre-retirees planning to retire in 15 years' time. They wanted to travel, however, they did not feel that they would be able to do so until retirement.

They completed their wish list and one of the items in the long-term section was a trip to New Zealand. As we want our clients to enjoy the journey, we put plans and structure in place for them to make New Zealand happen sooner.

A postcard arrived from New Zealand 18 months later with the comment "Thank you for giving us permission to take this holiday." Receiving that card was very powerful for me as it certainly demonstrated what can be achieved with direction and a different mindset. They have since been to Europe and have recently returned from a trip to Canada. In the meantime, the superannuation fund has been growing nicely to provide the lifestyle they desire in retirement.

Update – they retired last year. Woohoo!

Sixties and beyond – Patrick and Gail

Patrick and Gail retired at age 55 in 2002. At the time, Patrick had $410,000 and Gail had $255,000 accumulated in superannuation.

Since then, they have enjoyed a very comfortable lifestyle in retirement and travelled the world. At age 65 they were entitled to receive a part-Centrelink Aged Pension and we helped them complete the initial paperwork to apply. We liaise with Centrelink on their behalf to provide portfolio updates and required paperwork on an ongoing basis.

In retirement, the funds you have accumulated in your super can be rolled over to commence an income stream via an account-based pension (ABP).

Their funds are in individual ABPs, and since commencement, they have collectively taken pension/income payments totalling $547,000 and withdrawn a lump sum total of $114,500 (for holidays, a new car and other things). This equals a total of $661,500 that has been taken out of the collective 'pot' (at time of writing). This amount is more than they started with. Since age 60 this income has been tax-free.

Their current value at time of writing is $664,855.

As the fund does not pay any tax on earnings, they have received a total of $42,500 in refunds (retained within the ABPs).

They have learnt a lot about investing on their journey and feel very comfortable with the strategies we have applied over the years.

As a point of interest, their combined balances at the lowest point during the Global Financial Crisis was $467,500. They did not panic and stayed focused on the long term and felt comfortable with the level of diversification they had in their portfolios. They knew that the dividends were still coming in from the various sources within the funds and these were applied to buy more units at lower prices.

Since then they have withdrawn an additional $241,500 and as mentioned above the current value is $664,855. They are very happy that we remained firm with our long-term strategy.

Aged care – Susan

Susan had been a client for many years. As she grew older, her health began to fail. We were able to assist with all the complex financial rules and regulations associated with entering an aged care facility, while continuing to maximise her Centrelink Aged Pension entitlement.

She now receives the daily care she needs, and her family have peace of mind that her fees have been reduced due to the appropriate financial advice. Surplus funds also enable her to have her hair done every week and have access to other small luxuries, which ensure she is happy in her environment.

> "Action is the foundational
> key to all success."
>
> — Pablo Picasso

Are You Excited? Act Now!

In this chapter, we bring together all the pieces we have learnt regarding the health of your body, mind and finances.

In summary:

- ❦ Our attitude is determined by the positive or negative thoughts we think and the words we use daily.
- ❦ We are constantly sending messages to the world by the way we walk and the expressions we wear.
- ❦ Deep-seated emotions and negative beliefs could be impacting our enjoyment of life today and into the future.

ACTION

- 🙏 Abundance means different things to different people and we can be grateful for the many small pleasures that are available to us free of charge every day.
- 🙏 A wish list is one of the many tools available to help you achieve your goals and dreams.
- 🙏 With your recently acquired knowledge it is time to check off all the things on the homework list and start working towards a new chapter in your life.

Depending upon the complexity or simplicity of your wish list, the strategy that helps you achieve your goals and dreams may be very different. Individuals may be able to work along steadily with the knowledge they have gained. If not, professional help is only a phone call or email away.

What are the things you want to change in your life? This is the time to make choices that will affect the rest of your life. Each little step you take *today* will make a difference to all your *tomorrows*. It may seem overwhelming at first, however, just keep making those everyday choices and stay focused on where you want to be. Remember, yesterday is gone and tomorrow is ahead of us, yet today – this second, this minute, this hour – is what we have control over now!

> **A lot of energy can be lost hoping for a better past.**

A lot of energy can be lost hoping for a better past.

I have found that when I am faced with big stuff and feel overwhelmed, I just talk to myself and say, *Can I do this for the next 10/20/30 minutes?* Before long the task is well on its way. Then you can mentally (or physically) pat yourself on the back and say, "Well, that wasn't so bad – I can do another 20 minutes."

Now is the time to put into practice all that you have learnt in *Attitude, Abundance & Action*. It is time to make a difference in your own life *first*!

I wish you love, laughter and much happiness as you enjoy the journey and achieve your goals and dreams. I look forward to receiving your postcards and I hope this book will help you to create motivation, mindset and magic around money!

ATTITUDE, ABUNDANCE & ACTION

Find Out More

Congratulations on making your way through *Attitude, Abundance & Action*. Well done! 😊 I hope you have found clues, tips and words of wisdom to get you on track to a better future.

It never ceases to amaze me how people's lives can be changed, sometimes by just taking small incremental steps in the direction of their dreams. Changing your thoughts and attitude to be more positive and uplifting are powerful magnets to attract abundance into your life.

I have loved taking you on this journey. If you would like an Excel budget sheet or asset summary to help you get started, please go to our website www.goalsanddreams.com.au to access a copy.

If you are moving closer to retirement, we have a booklet called *Fear or Fun*. The idea for this came to me while in lockdown during COVID. I realised that I have all these wonderful clients who have been with me for 10, 15 or 20+ years. They were initially filled with doubts and concerns regarding what the future would look like and how would they manage life without the security of their regular wage. I came up with a number of questions and asked a selection of long-term clients if they would be willing to share their story and participate in the booklet. Fortunately, they all said yes. They answered questions like "Do you worry about money anymore?" or "Do you always have something to look forward to?"

My lovely clients have also shared many photos of their travels and adventures, which appear in this booklet. My clever daughter, Shelley, put it all together and now I share this with new clients who are planning and approaching retirement. If you would like a copy, please email aaa@goalsanddreams.com.au or visit our website www.goalsanddreams.com.au and we will send you a copy.

If you need someone to hold your hand and guide you on the pathway to a better future, either myself or one of my fantastic team will be happy to help. To book an initial complimentary phone call or meeting via Zoom/Teams or face to face, kindly visit our website or email reception@goalsanddreams.com.au or call (07) 3350 9595.

We would love to hear from you. If you feel so inclined, please send your feedback – or a postcard – to PO Box 130, Chermside South. QLD. 4032. Australia.

Goals & Dreams Financial Planning Pty Ltd

www.goalsanddreams.com.au

About the Author

Kath Orman Dip FP, CFP

For many years, Kath has been on the journey of self-development and growth, and she blends this knowledge with the practical application of financial planning.

Kath holds a Diploma of Financial Planning and is a Certified Financial Planner. She originally started in the industry in 1987 and has run her own financial planning business – Goals & Dreams Financial Planning Pty Ltd – since 2001.

Kath is also a Reiki healer and an angel intuitive and has written articles for the magazine *Holistic Bliss*. She has been a Transformologist® for the Un-Institute of Women™ as well as a Ringleader for Don Tolman, who teaches how the body can heal itself.

After much encouragement from her clients, industry professionals and other lightworkers, she has written *Attitude, Abundance & Action* for those who are ready and willing to make a difference in their own life first.

Kath has a holistic approach to financial planning and looks at where the client is now and where they want to be. She believes the most important issue is to enjoy the journey and find the balance in life.

She is passionate about helping her clients achieve their goals and dreams and is rewarded when clients send postcards from all over the world. These cards adorn an entire wall in the office reception area. When clients return from holidays, they are quick to visit to ensure their card has been displayed.

Resources

Books:

Chapman, G (2015), *The 5 Love Languages: The Secret to Love that Lasts*. Northfield Publishing, Chicago.

Covey, S.R (2020), *The 7 Habits of Highly Effective People*. Simon & Schuster, Sydney.

Furnham, A and Argyle, M (1998), *The Psychology of Money*. Routledge, London.

Videos:

Animated Book Summary – *The 7 Habits of Highly Effective People* by Stephen Covey
www.youtube.com/watch?v=ktlTxC4QG8g

Men's and Women's Brains
www.youtube.com/watch?v=AQ9L9YBJkk8

Stop It – Bob Newhart
https://www.youtube.com/watch?v=jvujypVVBAY

Websites:

Don Tolman – https://insightintoselfcare.com.au/don-tolman

Tyler Tolman – www.tylertolman.com

Un-Institute of Women™ – https://uninstituteofwomen.com

Marie Kondo – https://konmari.com

Robert Holden – www.robertholden.com

www.ingramcontent.com/pod-product-compliance
Lightning Source LLC
Chambersburg PA
CBHW050022130526
44590CB00042B/1668